LECTURES ON ECONOMIC PRINCIPLES

VOLUME III

By the same author

LECTURES ON
ECONOMIC PRINCIPLES

VOLUME III

SIR DENNIS H. ROBERTSON

Emeritus Professor of Political Economy in the University of Cambridge

> '*It's too late to correct it,*' *said the Red*
> *Queen:* '*when you've once said a thing,*
> *that fixes it, and you must take the*
> *consequences.*'
>
> THROUGH THE LOOKING-GLASS

STAPLES PRESS
LONDON

FIRST PUBLISHED 1959
REPRINTED 1960

Copyright © 1959
by Sir Dennis Robertson

VOLUME I FIRST PUBLISHED 1957
VOLUME II FIRST PUBLISHED 1958

This book is set in 'Monotype' Caslon Old Face series

Made and printed in Great Britain by
STAPLES PRINTERS LIMITED
at their Rochester, Kent, establishment

PREFACE

This final group of lectures dealt with more swiftly changing phenomena than its predecessors, and was subjected to more continuous and extensive revision. It is here reproduced substantially as it was delivered, for the last time, in the early summer of 1957; no attempt has been made either to bring the narrative up to date, or to revise the commentary, in the light of the somewhat spectacular happenings since that period.[1]

The overlaps with my previously published works are inevitably more frequent than in the preceding volumes. I must again apologise to any reader who may be irritated by re-encountering some passage (jokes and all) which has already met his eye; and again express my thanks to Messrs Allen & Unwin, the publishers of my book *Utility and All That*, for their indulgence in this matter, – mentioning now also in the same connection Messrs. Nisbet and Co., the publishers of my *Money*.

The summer term at Cambridge being shorter than the others, I have fattened out this volume by the inclusion of two addresses on cognate subjects delivered in the autumn respectively of 1956 and 1957.

D. H. R.

Cambridge,
December 1958

---

[1] The reader is asked to remember this particularly when he reaches page 134, where 'a few months ago' means 'a few months before May 1957'.

CONTENTS

I

MONEY IN A STABLE SOCIETY

Our analysis during the last two terms was mainly conducted on certain assumptions which, if you like, you can
call 'classical' or 'semi-classical', and of whose nature I
will briefly remind you. They were (apart from the
assumption of a closed system):

(1) Not that there is *no* money, but that money behaves
in such a way as faithfully to interpret the intentions of
those who make bargains and contracts in terms of it, and
not to distort them;

(2) Not that our community is stationary, but that the
growth of real income, whether due to a growth in the
quantity of the factors of production or to invention, etc.,
takes place more or less steadily and not by jerks – though
we deserted this assumption to some extent in studying
the short period theory of value and the associated complications in the theory of distribution;

(3) Not that there is *no* unemployment of resources,
but that there is a *tendency* to full employment, which can
however be thwarted not only by minor frictions of
various kinds, but by a decision by the owners of any
factor of production, whether on a sectional or a national
scale, to stick out for more than its economic price.

I have now therefore to say something about money,
about fluctuations in activity, about 'lapses from full employment' – the subject-matter of Marshall's projected
volume, never fully brought to birth, on 'Money, Credit
and Employment'.

If I may strike a personal note, this has always been to
me the most interesting part of economics – the only part
to which I can hope to be remembered as having made
any personal contribution. It is a source of regret to me

9

that I have to attempt to deal with it in a dozen lectures, and those squashed up into four weeks, so that I shall have to select and simplify rather drastically; and I need hardly say that in this field particularly the limitation of the analysis to a closed system means leaving out some of its most interesting aspects.

I regret too that some part of what I have to say is inevitably controversial, and critical of the work of my generous friend and brilliant teacher Maynard Keynes. There is no doubt that the modern concentration of interest on this range of subjects is due to him more than to any other single person. But if you have read any of my writings on these themes you will know already that I am definitely of opinion that in his later work Keynes, while he continued to contribute to, also marred by distortions and exaggerations of various kinds, a fruitful body of doctrine which had been being moulded over several decades by many hands. And if you have had time to look at the two studies by the eminent American economists John Williams and Howard Ellis in the *American Economic Review* (1948 and 1949), to which I referred you, you will know that I am not alone in that view. Nevertheless I am proud to have been Keynes's pupil, and to remember that, whatever he thought of our lack of receptivity to his later doctrines, he once in print described Hawtrey and myself as respectively his 'grandparent and parent in the paths of errancy'.

The first stage in our journey is, I think, to look a little more closely at the role of money in a more or less steady and serene economy. How shall we set about this? At the beginning of the Book of Common Prayer there is an excellent little essay entitled 'Of Ceremonies, why some be abolished and some retained'. It states, in words which seem to me to be singularly applicable to the economists of today, and doubtless of previous days, 'In this our time, the minds of men are so diverse that some think it is a great matter of conscience to depart from a piece of the least of their ceremonies, they be so addicted to their old customs: and again on the other hand some be so new-fangled that they would innovate all things and so despise the old that nothing can like them but that is new'; and it goes on to advocate a policy of the golden mean. You will have noticed a certain predilection on my part for the old customs: and I now invite you to approach with me the theory of money with the aid of an 'ancient ceremony', – the so-called 'Cambridge monetary equation', which makes the exchange *value* of money, considered as a special case of the general theory of value, the centre of the picture, and sets out the factors for discussion in a very simple and modest array of symbols. But I ought to remind you that this little formula has aroused the passionate scorn of some modern writers, one of whom[1] even appears to attribute to its use the unfortunate inability of economists to predict the future accurately – a rather optimistic view, for I am afraid the event has shown that the difficulties of prediction lie deeper than in the use of this or that little piece of apparatus!

In its most disarming and non-committal form the Cambridge equation runs $M = KRP$. Let us examine the letters in order. M is the number of units of money in existence, and at once brings us up against the question of definition – what do we mean by Money? Some barren controversies – I allude here to old controversies rather than recent ones – could have been avoided if it had been more clearly realised that we habitually use the word in two senses – an abstract scale of measurement and a concrete means of discharging obligations. The former, an abstract 'money of account', is logically independent of, and perhaps historically anterior to, the latter; since it can quite well co-exist with a system of barter, and perhaps could also co-exist with a universal system of payment by

[1] Mrs Robinson, *Review of Economic Studies*, Vol. I, p. 24.

cancellation of book debts, in which no concrete money, even of the most tenuous kind, passed from hand to hand. The confusion is rendered easier by the fact that early scales were generally in terms of some commodity; thus the Homeric ox was perhaps never really used as a coin but only as a scale. Later, especially when the State takes over control, the scale tends to lose any commodity significance it ever had. Some modern scale-units are relics of old commodity-scales – e.g. the English 'pound' – of silver; others, e.g. the various Continental 'crowns', are purely fancy units.

Realisation of this double use of the word money leads us to the neat fourfold classification of the functions of money given by Marshall (*M.C.C.*, p. 16, n.).

	Abstract sense	*Concrete sense*
Immediate use	Common scale of values	Medium of exchange
Deferred use	Standard of debts	Store of value

As regards immediate uses, money, by facilitating exchange, promotes economic freedom – specialisation of productive function on the one hand, maximisation of consuming power on the other. I needn't enlarge on this – the textbooks are full of the agonies of the two men, one with a spare fish, the other with a spare pair of boots, vainly seeking one another. For a modern variant, see Radford's vivid account (*Economica*, November 1945) of the evolution of a cigarette-currency in a prisoners-of-war camp. Historically the process of 'adaeration' is closely connected with the development of division of labour; and experience shows that people will stick to the use of money even when it is rapidly depreciating, because of the inconvenience of barter. Moneyless communism, compelling people to take their allotted real income in certain forms or not at all, is prima facie wasteful; though of course there is a partial place for it in special circumstances, e.g. in army life.

As regards deferred uses, the possession of money, as contrasted with a stock of some specific good, helps to give the individual security and freedom of manoeuvre. Money also immensely facilitates the making of savings and the transfer of command over capital. As a result, the provision of a medium of exchange has become inextricably tangled up, in subtle ways, with the market for loans – an entanglement which has been the source of many of the main difficulties, both theoretical and practical, of the whole subject.

To return to the equation. Here M stands for money in the concrete quantitative sense. The question thus arises, how wide shall we cast our net of definition? I am in favour of casting it fairly widely, and defining money as anything which is generally, or even widely, acceptable in payment for goods or discharge of other obligations. That means that, for the kind of community in which we are most interested, we must include deposits with a bank drawable on by cheque (and therefore exclude coins, etc., held by banks, i.e. our M is money in the hands of 'the public'); and I doubt whether it is convenient to try, as is sometimes done, to draw the line at 'current accounts' (U.K.) or 'demand deposits' (U.S.A.), on which a cheque can be drawn without notice, excluding 'deposit accounts' (U.K.) or 'time deposits' (U.S.A.), for operating on which notice is at any rate nominally required. On the other hand it would be attractive if it were feasible, which it isn't, to frame our definition so that it would be unaffected by the technical difference between cases in which bank advances are made by way of loan in the strict sense, the borrower being credited with the funds forthwith and spending them as he needs them, and those in which they are made by way of extension of overdraft facilities, no money coming into existence till a cheque is drawn and used by the borrower. As it is, we must remember that different amounts of money in existence will be associated with a given business situation according to which of these practices exists. Note in passing that our definition does not make the non-yielding of interest an essential characteristic of money; if, as was common 150 years ago, an interest-bearing bill of exchange is circulating in payment for goods, or if, as was the case in this country till quite recently, a customer is able to obtain some bank interest even on a current account, that does not prevent the thing in question from being 'money'.

What has determined the amount of money in existence, that is to say in the hands of the public, in the community under examination? That question cannot be answered in any particular case without a detailed historical and institutional study, such as falls outside the scope of these lectures. Putting the matter in the broadest terms, we may say that M has been determined by the interplay, at various preceding dates, of the actions of at least three parties. First, the producers of precious metals, who have in effect put money into existence by *spending* it, though under modern conditions this is a highly stylised account of their influence. Secondly the banks, who learnt early in their history how to put money into existence by *lending* it to the public or exchanging it for income-yielding assets. Thirdly the Government, which has operated in the course of history in three ways. (i) It has made decisions about the monetary standard, i.e. about how many units of money the lumps of metal put into the machine by the metal-producers shall be worth. (ii) By a great variety of devices and with greater or less success, acting sometimes directly and sometimes through the agency of a more or less independent Central Bank, it has sought to exercise control, both in an upward and in a downward direction, over the number of monetary units created and kept in existence by the banks in the course of their dealings with the public. (iii) It has itself put money into existence by spending and taken it out of existence by taxation, sometimes directly and sometimes by arranging for banks to create money by lending to itself and to destroy money by accepting repayment from itself.

A government can limit its own powers over the money supply by declaring its adhesion to an external standard. Thus the best answer that can be given to the vexed question, 'What is a gold standard?', is perhaps that any country may be said to have a gold standard which is making persistent and effective arrangements to keep approximately constant the value of its monetary unit in terms of gold. But it is not really a very satisfying answer: for experience shows that even when such arrangements exist they do not always *play the dominant part* in governing decisions about the size of the money supply. The monetary history of the inter-war period is largely the history of the development of devices for increasing the elements of 'play' in the supply of money which have always existed to some extent even in countries operating a metallic standard; and under the new gold standard, if we like to call it so, set up by the Bretton Woods Agreement, these elements of 'play' have continued, and seem likely to continue, to be large.

Ought we to add a fourth party, namely the money-using public, to those already listed as determining between them the volume of the money supply? At first sight it would seem so; for certainly the public can take the initiative in *reducing* the money supply by using its balances to repay loans to the banks, or to buy securities from the banks, or in some conditions direct from the Government. But the banks and the Government have it in their power to counter the public's action in various ways; and while a quarrel and a baby are not the only things which it takes two to make, the most illuminating approximation to the complicated truth is probably still reached by regarding the supply of money in a western country as being determined by the Government, or rather – for Central Banks are not everywhere yet mere 'creatures' – by the Monetary Authority: subject on the one hand to autonomous vagaries of varying degrees of importance on the part of the ordinary banks, and on the other to self-imposed limitations, of varying degrees of stringency, as regards adherence to an external standard. I do not think the important articles by Sayers and others which I have listed, and about which I shall say a little more later, really constrain us to alter this broad generalisation.

That is as far down this street as my timetable permits me to wander. But I beg of you not to despise monetary history; for I am sure that the monetary policy of nations is often unintelligible without some understanding of the queer institutional jungles out of which it has sprung. In particular, it is of importance that so much of the world's money appears in some balance-sheet or other as a 'liability' balanced by an 'asset'. This gives rise to absurd happenings, as when the monetary rot in Germany in 1924 was stopped by the issue of a new note, the rentenmark, which was described as being 'based on' the soil of Germany; or when Roosevelt issued a new emergency note in the crisis of March 1933 'against' Government bonds and commercial paper, and described it as 'sound currency, because backed by actual good assets'. Indeed, we need look no farther than our own country, and I invite you to look up the scrap of Platonic dialogue analysing the immediately pre-war British monetary system which is reprinted in my *Essays*, pp. 158–9. But things which are absurd are not on that account unimportant, even if there were no justification, as in fact there is, for the deep-seated instinct of the public, even in Anglo-Saxon lands and far more markedly in others, to ask from time to time what lies 'behind' its money.

Turning to the other side of the equation, R is the real national output or income of goods – including capital goods – and services per unit of time, say a year, and P its price. These symbols therefore raise all those 'index-number' difficulties about the measurement of the movements of the volume and value of composite flows which I dealt with briefly in connection with the concept of national income, and which I cannot pursue further. But it is important to observe that $\frac{1}{P}$ is the value of money *in terms of final output*, which, even so far as it can be made precise, is only one of several possible meanings of the value of money. I shall confine my treatment to this meaning, though if my scope of operations permitted I should not. For monetary theory has become poorer as well as richer as a result of the growing concentration in recent years on the concept of national income; and there is much to be learnt from older discussions of the value of money in terms of other and broader categories of economic objects, and particularly from the divergences which occur in periods of change between the movements of the prices of final goods as sold to the public and those of the prices of intermediate products – raw materials and goods at wholesale – which are more subject to the influence of changes in expectation, and hence more volatile. (Some aspects of this subject of the relation between different price-levels are dealt with, if anyone is interested, in the latter part of No. VI of my *Essays*.)

So we reach the last symbol K, the Prince of Denmark in the Hamlet of the Cambridge equation, and define it as the proportion of its annual real income which the community wishes to keep enough money to purchase – or, if you like, over which it wishes to keep command in the form of money. This proportion is of course a weighted average of the little k's of the various economic subjects, to be interpreted as including business firms as well as individuals, of which the community is made up. In handling this concept of the k of the individual, whether regarded as a private person or as the head of a business, there are two important points to grasp which may help to make it more palatable. First, it is not necessary to suppose that he himself thinks in real terms; to him, k is simply the proportion of his *money* stock to his *money* income. Secondly, it is not necessary to suppose that he is arriving at decisions about the size of his money stock solely by reference to the size of his income – he may well be considering also the size of his total wealth or of his total annual turnover. But, however *arrived at*, it can be *expressed* as a proportion of income. And in my view it is not irrelevant or improper, as Keynes argued in the *Treatise on Money* when he was still interested in this range of questions, thus to express the community's whole money-stock as a proportion of its income, but the very reverse, since the whole of the stock is *potentially* expendable against real income or output, and if in any short period of time a larger or smaller proportion of it were to be thus expended, very important consequences would ensue. (This point is discussed in the first part, pp. 93–4, of No. VI of my *Essays* just referred to, and is worth, I think, looking at even by those who don't want to bother about the second part.)

Thus we reach our equation $M = KRP$, which can be read as follows: In a stable community the quantity of money in existence is also that which people wish to hold, having regard to the level of output, its price level, and their preferences as regards the form in which they hold their resources.

Now, before delving more deeply into the nature of K, let us put the equation into another dress. Assuming first that all real income changes hands with the aid of money, the equation can be written in the form $MV = RP$, where V is the reciprocal of K. The equation now refers not to a point of time, but to a period of time, say (as before) a year, V being the number of times each unit of money on the average changes hands against the constituents of real income during the period. This way of putting things, while less fundamental than the other, has a longer history, and has its conveniences, since V is an entity which, if statistics were good enough, could be directly measured, while K is an entity which can only be inferred.

But there is a trap. In a community in which a perceptible proportion of real income is not changing hands at all, or is changing hands by means of some kind of barter or direct offset, V, the recorded (or rather, in principle recordable) velocity of circulation of money against real income, will not be equal to $\frac{1}{K}$ but to something less. For the equation representing the flow of money against real income becomes $MV = (1 - Q)RP$, while our original equation is still $M = KRP$, whence $V = \frac{1 - Q}{K}$.

Now let us return to $M = KRP$, and probe more deeply into K. Why do people want to keep part of their resources in the form of money? The answer is often summed up in a single phrase, 'out of a desire for liquidity'. But these physical metaphors in economics are tricky things – I once read in the *Economist* an account of the position of the French banks, not long after a crisis had occurred, which ended up, 'In fact the banks are now once more in a thoroughly solid and liquid condition.' So perhaps we had better look a little closer. Following a somewhat crabbed article by Makower and Marschak (*Economica*, August 1938), I invite you to distinguish, within the general notion of liquidity, at least three separate elements. The first is assumed *safety*, i.e. immunity from the risk of varying returns, some of which may be negative, which attaches to the holding of most forms of property. The second is the *convenience* – the avoidance of cost, both financial and psychic – which is conferred by holding a certain amount of a thing which, by definition, is generally acceptable, instead of having to get hold of it in small quantities at short notice. The third, which is not quite the same, may be called *saleability* – you can rely on disposing of money, just because of its general acceptability, in a perfect market, which you cannot do with a house or a picture. It is above all this quality which gives the holder of money what I have called freedom of manoeuvre, and which clings to money even when it has manifestly lost 'safety' in an inflation.

It is necessary to remind you that all these qualities are quite distinct from that quality of being expected, in certain circumstances, to rise in value in terms of a particular type of asset, namely gilt-edged securities, to which Keynes has, as I think unfortunately, specially attached the term liquidity in the formulation of his theory of the rate of interest, to which I shall return later.

With such notions in our head, we can go on to tabulate, in as much or as little detail as we please, the factors governing the magnitude of K in a relatively stable society. In pursuit of my enforced policy of condensation, I shall be content to divide them into five groups, without further elaboration. We have:

(1) Factors connected with business habits – the frequency and regularity with which payments are made, and so forth;

(2) Factors connected with the structure of industry – in particular how far the production and sale of output are split up into stages in the hands of different firms between whom payments have to be made for the transfer of goods in process or in store;

(3) The general conditions of social and business life, and hence the degree of certainty and confidence with which consumers and producers are making their plans – once more, our 'stable' economy is not to be conceived of as a frozen one from which all individual uncertainty has been expelled;

(4) The state of development of the markets for existing capital goods – land, houses, etc., and of paper titles thereto: this works both ways, – such things need money to exchange them with, but some of them are also partial substitutes for money;

(5) The rate of return obtainable by employing resources otherwise than by tying them up in the form of money. In connection with this, it is, perhaps, once more necessary to remind you that the purchase of gilt-edged securities is by no means the only, or normally the most economically important, alternative use of resources to holding money.

Pursuing this line of thought, we may find it convenient, even in considering a 'stable' economy, to divide the stock of money in thought into two parts, active and inactive. In one sense, indeed, *all* money is inactive except when it is actually passing from one person to another; but in another sense that part of it may fairly be thought of as active which is required as a minimum to implement the existing flow of payments and receipts of all kinds, and that part as inactive which is held in reserve to meet more or less dimly foreseen risks or take advantage of more or less dimly foreseen opportunities. It is the size of the latter rather than the former which is susceptible to my fifth factor, i.e. the competing attractions of other uses of resources. But it is not easy to draw a clear line even conceptually, much less statistically (in respect of bank deposits, the distinction cannot be regarded as corresponding at all accurately with that between deposit and current accounts (U.K.) or time and demand deposits (U.S.A.)).

A word on another matter of terminology will be in place at this point. A person who in any period takes steps to increase the proportion existing at the beginning of that period of his money stock to his money income can conveniently be said to be 'hoarding', and a person who does the opposite to be 'dishoarding'. By so acting, he cannot of course in most cases increase or decrease the total stock of money; but he *can* increase or decrease the inactive stock at the expense or to the benefit of the active stock. And by diminishing or augmenting the flow of money directed to the purchase of final output he can also, in certain circumstances, increase or diminish the real value of the *total* stock of money. We shall have to look into these processes more closely later, but I should like to put on record at this point my inability to understand the dislike which Keynes and some of his expositors have displayed of this harmless little word 'hoarding', which seems to me excellently adapted to express in nontechnical language the type of change to which I have applied it.

We must now turn to a more substantial question. What is the relation of the 'demand for money' in the sense we have been examining to the ordinary concept of demand, and in particular to the proposition that the value of a thing measures its marginal utility to the purchaser or possessor? We must picture the individual distributing his real income between the uses of immediate consumption, of adding to his income-bearing property and of adding to his store of ready value in such wise as to make equal the marginal utility derived from each use. Or taking a more static view we can picture him as distributing his *stock* of real resources between income-bearing property and a store of ready value so that its marginal utility in each use is equal.

Never let us forget the alternative of *consumption*: nevertheless for the moment we will ignore it, in order to get a two-dimensional picture.

In Fig. (i) total resources AC are distributed so that AB = CE. OC is the same as *KR* in the equation, and once it is determined constitutes a fixed demand for money in terms of real things. If we want to represent it as a schedule

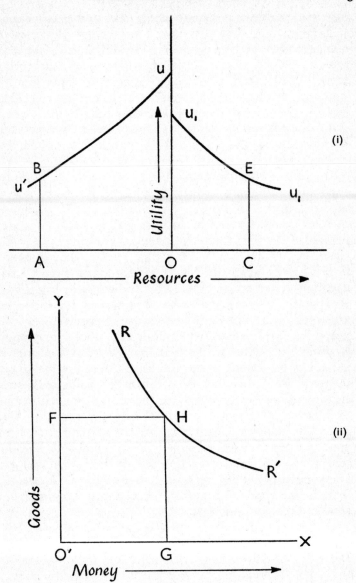

or curve, measuring money along $O'X$ and goods along $O'Y$ (Fig. (ii)), then the curve must be our old friend a rectangular hyperbola; so $FO'GH = OC = KR$. But it is the curve $U_iU'_i$ that is really of interest − i.e. it is not to money itself that the concept of marginal utility is relevant, but to resources devoted to the monetary use. This has not always been realised; attempts have been made to connect marginal utility with money itself, for instance by representing the marginal utility of money as tied up in some way with those transactions which, having regard to the existing supply of money, it is just worth while to conduct with money instead of by barter. All such lines of thought, in my judgment, lead into bog.

The truism enshrined in Fig. (ii) is sometimes expressed by saying that the demand for money has an elasticity of one; but I think that phrase, though sanctioned by Marshall and Pigou, is best avoided (so I have used any letter rather than D for the curve in Fig. (ii)). As Patinkin[1] has lately been dinning into us, in the proper sense of the phrase the elasticity of demand of the individual, and hence of the public as a whole, for money is probably normally less than one. A man whose real income is unchanged, but who finds the real value of his money stock diminished by a fall in the value of money (rise in prices) will, indeed, cut down his expenditure in order to expand his money stock; but he probably will not try to expand it to the full extent of the rise, i.e. he will, as a result of his impoverishment, probably be content to hold a rather smaller real balance than before. Conversely, of course, for a move in the opposite direction. This is illustrated in Fig. (iii), where the rectangle OL is smaller than the rectangle OQ.

So far we have been using our equation simply as a peg on which to hang discussion of its constituent elements. But I do not doubt myself that for the stable economy we

[1] *Money, Interest and Prices*, pp. 41–5, 103–4.

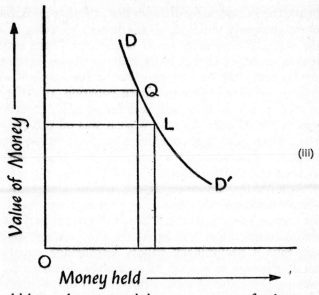

(iii)

have hitherto been examining we can go further, and write it in the form $\frac{1}{P} = \frac{KR}{M}$ – this form conveying the suggestion that the value of money $\left(\frac{1}{P}\right)$, like that of other things, can fairly be said to be determined by the forces of demand and supply, and is in effect the link through which the decision of the public as to how much money it wants to hold, and the decision of the Monetary Authority as to how much money there is to be, are kept in harmony with one another. For in comparing such stable economies there seems no reason to assume the degree of employment of resources to be greater in one than in the other, while they may differ in many other relevant respects. To give just one instance: if, in two otherwise similar societies A and B, K is smaller in A than in B owing to business being more closely integrated and less money therefore held up in taking care of intermediate payments between firms, the price-level will be higher in A than in B. So even more obviously will it if, all the factors affecting K being the same, R is smaller or M is greater. There seems no reason to doubt that it is for reasons of this kind, which are looked after by one or other of the symbols on the right-hand side of our rewritten equation, that the value of money, e.g. in England, is different today from what it was in the Middle Ages or what it was on the eve of the 1914 War. And that conclusion would, I think, alone be sufficient justification for starting our study with this antique piece of furniture.

Admittedly, however, if we try to analyse a more volatile situation with its aid, we have to be on the look-out for certain complications. I have not yet finished with the stable community; but let us for the moment desert it, and take a preliminary gallop, Cambridge equation in hand, through a period of monetary disturbance. Still making the value of money in terms of output the centre of the picture, we may note three main complications:

(i) The demand for money is found not to be independent of the supply. Thus suppose there has been an increase in supply, due to a change of policy on behalf of the banks, which raises prices and profits; this increases the attractiveness of the use of resources in direct investment, thus reducing K and generating a further rise in prices and profits. The extreme case of this reaction is an inflation of the money supply by Government, as in 1922 Germany or 1944 Hungary, leading to a 'flight into commodities' and a rise in prices much exceeding the increase in M. Conversely, a contraction of the money supply, as achieved by Belgium in 1945, or even the cessation of a process of increase, steadies up K, and may lead to a fall in prices greater in proportion than any actual contraction which has occurred in M.

(ii) The supply of money is found not to be independent of the demand. Thus suppose there has been a rise of confidence in the prospects of business which diminishes K, so increasing the money demand for output and raising prices and profits. Then the banks may be induced to increase their loans in order to enable some traders to finance the old volume of trade at the new prices, or the Government itself may procure the creation of additional money in its favour in order to pay its increased bills. Thus fuel is added to the flames. In the converse case, if prices fall and traders in consequence find themselves with redundant money and seek to repay their bank loans, the banks may be unable or unwilling to counteract the effect which such repayments have in reducing M. Thus in either case the money supply may prove itself *perversely elastic* – a fall in the value of money leading to a relaxation in the conditions of supply and a rise in its value to their tightening up.

(iii) In so far as the prices either of final goods or of productive services are 'administered', i.e. are not plastic under the impulse of demand or the stress of competition, the effect of a change in the money-stream $\frac{M}{K}$ will be registered in changes of R rather than of P. Remembering our short-period theory of value of particular commodities, we can extend it to output as a whole by saying that if wages and some other costs are rigid, but there is active competition between firms, output will tend to be adjusted up or down to the point at which marginal prime cost is brought into equality with price. And we can then modify that result by saying that, in so far as firms – in manufacture, at all events – are apt to behave more monopolistically in bad times than in good, contraction of output in face of compression of demand may well be carried beyond this point. This, however, is a 'short-period equilibrium' result which may never be attained in the hugger-mugger of the kind of cumulative movement we are now considering; for I should like to remind you once more of the danger of reasoning as though short-period equilibrium were always, or indeed perhaps ever, established any more than long-period equilibrium is. What is however true and important is that in any but a very short time-interval some effect of an increase in M or diminution of K may be exercised in increasing R, thus raising the demand for money and checking the fall in its value: and conversely in the opposite case of an increase of K or diminution of M.

Does it follow, as it is sometimes said to do, that the Cambridge equation, in such periods of cumulative change, loses all usefulness as an instrument of analysis? I do not myself think so, if our analysis of causes is being conducted with a view to a search for cures. For one thing it may serve to remind us that even the level of rigid or 'administered' prices of goods or productive services is not arrived at out of the blue, but has some relation with the behaviour of M, K, and R in the past and in the expected future; and under sufficient pressure from the stream of money demand it may break down – more easily in the upward, but sometimes also in the downward, direction. For another thing, it may remind us that while at any moment M may have been behaving passively in the past, the power of governments to catch hold and make it behave actively is often greater than they choose to believe. In other words, while a given change or movement in prices may come about, if you like so to put it, 'spontaneously', a given behaviour of M is an essential condition for the change or movement to be maintained, and if some other behaviour of M takes place the change will be inhibited or reversed. The more we think in terms of logical dependence rather than mere chronological sequence, the less reason we shall find to quarrel with formulations which exhibit P as the final or resultant term of the story. The whole notion of causation, in economics as elsewhere, is a difficult one, and I agree with Howard

Ellis, who at the end of an excellent discussion of the matter in his (somewhat misnamed) book, *German Monetary Theory* (p. 195), ends by saying, 'For purposes of economic control, if the development may be partly managed through the "essential condition", it would be over(ly) fastidious not to regard the condition pragmatically as a cause.' Those European governments which in 1945 or later took drastic action on the supply of money in order to check a runaway movement of prices have provided fresh evidence for the validity of this way of looking at things.

But finally, while in some ways governments have more power than they like to think, in others they have less; and the Cambridge equation furnishes us with a constant reminder of how, in a community which has not lost all economic freedom, the incalculable K of the public hangs like the sword of Damocles over the head of many amiable and ambitious schemes.

Well that, you may say, is a lot to get out of four letters – in Mrs Robinson's witty phrase 'we have been telling the equation what is happening, it has not been telling us'. But nobody, I think, has ever expected a little group of symbols to be a *substitute* for an argument! And to my mind one of the attractive features of the Cambridge equation is precisely that which rouses Mrs Robinson's ire, namely its complete generality, so that we can use it to order our thoughts about a great number of different sequences of events, some of them starting at one point in the causal chain and some at another – in some of them the rate of interest playing a prominent part and in others not. For while I find it convenient to defer what I have to say about the rate of interest in connection with these cumulative movements, I should like to protest in passing against a view to which Mrs Robinson has given countenance on p. 97 of her little book, but which Wicksell himself, the pioneer of this line of thought, was at pains to disclaim – namely that no piece of monetary reasoning into which the rate of interest is not dragged by the heels has any validity at all!

My conclusion then is that the 'ancient ceremony' of the Cambridge equation should be retained!

APPENDIX TO CHAPTER I
Sundry References

Neo-classics

MARSHALL. *Money, Credit and Commerce* (referred to as *M.C.C.*), Book I, ch. IV, and pp. 73–6 and 254–8.

—— *Official Papers*, pp. 48–52, 130–1, 270–4.

WICKSELL. *Interest and Prices.*

—— *Lectures on Political Economy*, Vol. II, ch. 4.

HAWTREY. *Art of Central Banking*, chs. 3 and 5.

Some comments on Keynes

HABERLER. *Prosperity and Depression*, Part I, ch. 8.

HAWTREY. *Capital and Employment*, ch. 7.

LANGE. 'Rate of Interest [etc.]', *Economica*, February 1938, and *Readings in Business Cycle Theory*, No 8

WILLIAMS. Article in *American Economic Review*, May 1948, No. 2, p. 253.

ELLIS. Article in *American Economic Review*, March 1949, p. 465.

ROBERTSON. *Essays in Monetary Theory* (referred to as *Essays*), Nos. 1, 8, 9, 11.

—— *Utility and All That*, Nos. 5 and 6.

—— Interchange with H. Johnson, *Review of Economic Studies*, No. 49 (1951–2), pp. 90–110.

Recent studies of British monetary system

SAYERS. 'The Determination of the volume of bank deposits in England, 1955–6' (No. 8 of *Central Banking after Bagehot*).

W.M.D. 'The Floating Debt Problem', *Lloyds Bank Review*, April 1956.

W.T.C.K. 'Should Liquidity Ratios be prescribed?', *The Banker*, April 1956.

The Trade Cycle

HABERLER. *Prosperity and Depression*, chs. 10, 11, 13.

SCHUMPETER. No. 1 of *Readings in Business Cycle Theory*.

HICKS. *The Trade Cycle.*

HANSEN. *Business Cycles and National Income*, Part III.

ROBERTSON. *Economic Commentaries*, No. V.

THE MEANING OF MONETARY EQUILIBRIUM

That was no more than a preliminary gallop through a period of monetary disturbance. Now let us go back to the stable economy, and address ourselves to a very fundamental question. What exactly is the behaviour of money which we are assuming when we analyse the working of a stable economy? Or, more normatively, how should a Monetary Authority act in order to preserve monetary equilibrium, that is, to keep a stable economy stable?

Now there are various kinds of stable economy. We need not at this point go so far back – or forward – in thought as to examine a stable economy which is also *stationary*. It seems more natural to start with one which is undergoing steady and harmonious *growth*, i.e. one in which all the factors of production are growing by *x* per cent per unit of time, without any fundamental change occurring in habits or technique. This perhaps puts a little strain on our intellectual consciences in respect of 'land', which by definition is a factor which does not grow: but I think we shall do well to stifle this objection, realising that at best we can only make approximations to the complex truth by the use of simplified models. Under such conditions, then, the prima facie duty – we had better not put it higher – of the Monetary Authorities in a closed system would be to cause the total flow of money income, and hence, if K is unchanging, the stock of money, to grow in the same ratio. If they did this successfully, their success could be, and has been by various writers, described in three ways, all of which appear to come to very much the same thing.

(i) They are ensuring 'neutrality' on the part of money

– not in the sense that its use makes no difference to economic life, which would of course be at a much lower level if it were deprived of the use of money, but in the sense that it does not introduce disturbing or dislocating factors, but permits and assists the real underlying forces making for general equilibrium, as expressed in the theories of value and distribution, to work themselves out.

(ii) They are preserving a 'normal' level of profits, i.e. that level which is required, in a free enterprise economy, to stimulate the given rate of growth in the aggregate of material capital and business organisation. Since the rewards of the hired factors are fixed, for shorter or longer periods, in terms of money, a more rapid growth of the income-stream would generate windfall profits, and a less rapid one windfall losses. The former would stimulate attempts to increase the total volume of production, though we assume that in the condition of steady growth in which we start there is little play for such further increase, all resources being fairly fully employed. But such a swelling of the income-stream would also, if the Monetary Authority were acting through a banking system, change the *character* of production in the direction of consisting more largely of instrumental goods. For the easier terms of lending associated with the swollen money supply would give a special encouragement to production for distant ends. In an integrated economy this would show itself in a tendency on the part of each firm to devote more of its energies to making instruments; in a differentiated one, to a relative rise in the price of instruments, thus attracting more enterprise and other resources to their manufacture. *Per contra* an expansion of money income at a rate lower than x per cent per period would tend both to a change in the character of output in the opposite direction to that described, and also to a reduction in the rate of growth, and perhaps even in the absolute level, of the *total* output of the community.

(iii) They are preserving equilibrium in the market for thrift. In spite of the fact that the banks are perpetually creating additional money by way of loan and investment, they are not distorting the market for investable funds by doing so, but are simply bringing to fruition the thrifty intentions of the growing community. If they failed to create additional money they would be allowing these thrifty intentions to go to waste, partly in the form of uncovenanted consumption by the members of the community with fixed money incomes, partly in the form of idleness of productive resources. *Per contra*, if they were to create money at a more rapid rate, they would be outrunning the thrifty intentions of the community; the enhanced rate of growth of fixed capital would be being provided out of what have been aptly called 'forced levies' imposed on those with fixed or sticky money incomes for the benefit of the entrepreneur class. And for completeness I must add, without pursuing the concept further at the moment, that in this third way of describing the criterion of 'monetary equilibrium' it can be said that the rate of interest is being held continuously at its 'normal' or 'natural' level, instead of being caused or allowed to rise above or fall below it.

It is this third way of looking at the criterion of 'monetary equilibrium', namely in terms of equilibrium in the market for thrift, which after playing, since the days of Wicksell, a very fruitful part in the development of Swedish, Austrian and English thought on these matters, ran in the 1930s into terminological troubles which generated a good deal of heat and have not yet been wholly exorcised. In those days it was suggested in effect by some writers that the criterion is meaningless, since in any unit of time the volume of money savings is always and inevitably equal to the money value of the addition made to real capital, nowadays commonly labelled investment. For, so runs the argument, each of these quantities is equal to the total of money income less the money paid out for the purchase of, i.e. the money received from the sale of, consumption goods. Thus, for instance, whatever the banks do about the creation of money, they are inevitably acting merely as faithful intermediaries for the marketing of savings; if the result of their actions is to speed up, or damp down, the creation of real capital, the volume of saving inevitably expands, or contracts, to match. To quote from a distinguished convert to this way of thinking, Lord Beveridge,[1] 'capital expenditure itself brings into existence the very savings necessary to finance it'.

Now truisms are often very noble animals; but I must confess that this particular truism – that, if defined so as to be identical, money savings and money investment are indeed equal – has always seemed to me very unilluminating. As I have said in print, if we are going to state it at all, I would prefer to state it in a less pretentious and less tendencious form, such as this: All money which is anywhere must indeed be somewhere. The most profligate expenditure by a belligerent government – for government deficits count as honorary investment in this connection – brings into existence the very savings necessary to finance it in the sense that *some* poor devil is always holding each of the million-pengo notes, or whatever they may be, which have been poured out on to the markets.

The instinct of serious economic writers to get behind this tautology and to find a form of words which will satisfactorily express monetary equilibrium in terms of what is happening in the capital market has proved persistent and deep, and after the flurry of the 1930s is now re-asserting itself in the literature. Let me remind you briefly of some of its earlier manifestations. Hawtrey (see *Capital and Employment*, pp. 160 ff.) has confined himself to emphasising the distinction between active or designed investment

---

[1] *Full Employment in a Free Society*, p. 337.

and passive or undesigned investment, which takes the form of an increase in the stocks of unsold goods. Savings, in Hawtrey's treatment, are necessarily equal to the sum of the two, but not to the active investment alone; and if they are not so equal, that is a sign of disequilibrium. The Swedish writers have felt, rightly in my opinion, the need for extending this distinction between active and passive to savings as well as to investment. Thus if, at the end of a given short interval of time, I find my money balances unexpectedly increased as a result of expansionist activity on the part, say, of the banks, this increment of balances may indeed be called actual or realised savings, but must be distinguished in thought from the savings which I had planned to make at the outset of the time-interval, and which alone can be treated functionally, i.e. regarded as depending on some variable such as income or the rate of interest in accordance with some intelligible psychological law. But this distinction between 'ex-post' and 'ex-ante' savings, as the Swedes call them, does not of itself, as might at first be thought, afford us a firm basis for a criterion of monetary equilibrium. For suppose, in an economy hitherto stable, the public as a whole rightly anticipates an abnormal expansion, or a contraction, in the money income stream, and expands or contracts its ex-ante savings to match; then ex-ante and ex-post savings will remain equal to one another and to realised investment in spite of the disequilibrating expansion or contraction of the income-stream. I think myself that to find a concept of 'savings' in which their divergence from investment can be treated as a criterion of disequilibrium we must have recourse to a device by which the savings of one period are regarded as the excess, over the consumption of that period, of the income received not in that but in the preceding period. This is the method which I adopted thirty years ago in my *Banking Policy and the Price Level* and elaborated later in my 'Saving and Hoarding' (*Essays,*

No. 4); and I think I can claim that, in spite of the formidable difficulties in the way of making precise the
conception of a 'period', it is now finding increasing
favour, certainly in America and even in England – even
perhaps in Cambridge! I do not think any writer would
write now those sentences to which, though one could
parallel them from Keynes's own writings and those of
Harrod and others, I still feel constrained to point as the
locus classicus of the confusion which bedevilled discussion
of these matters for so long. 'If,' wrote Mrs Robinson,[1] in
explaining how the outlay on building a new house
generates further expenditure and further income in successive 'rounds' – 'if the whole outlay on house-building
were added to saving at the first round there would be no
second round': forgetting, apparently, that according to
the definition given a few pages earlier the whole outlay
has inevitably been 'added to saving' at the first round.
And again, 'the increase in incomes must necessarily continue up to the point at which there is an addition to saving
equal to the additional outlay on house-building'. But
on her definition this point is reached instantaneously,
whether there is any increase in incomes beyond the
original outlay on house-building or whether there is
none!

There is as yet, I am afraid, no standard terminology in
these matters. But I am glad to notice that the authors of
Government White Papers are now at some pains to make
plain to their readers the non-significance of that annually
recurring equality between the recorded totals of saving
and of capital outlay which to some early readers of the
series, in search of evidence of the size of the 'inflationary
gap' about which they had been told, seemed so miracu-
lous and so reassuring. Nowadays these writers not
infrequently permit themselves to speak of 'genuine'
saving or 'voluntary' saving, though they have not yet

[1] *Introduction to the Theory of Employment*, p. 22.

committed themselves to a term for its opposite. And I was delighted to read in the Economic Survey for 1949 (p. 45) that 'if . . . incomes can be kept at a steady level and savings can be matched with investment, financial stability can be maintained'. I dare say you can hardly realise with what a howl of derision that very sensible little sentence would have been greeted only ten years earlier. 'Poor fellow,' it would have been said, 'hasn't he heard that savings are always matched with investment? Why even —— knows that now.' If you think I am flogging a dead horse, please look up the *Economic Journal* for March 1947, p. 40, where, in Professor Robinson's excellent obituary notice of Lord Keynes, you will find it suggested that in 1930 mankind still moved in darkness because this great discovery, that things defined as identical are indeed equal, had not yet been made.

Perhaps, even if (like myself) with some reservations, most economists *would* now more or less agree on some such formulation as this, that equality of designed or intended savings with designed or intended capital outlay is one way of expressing the condition of equilibrium. Indeed, in a manner specially appropriate to the case which we started out to discuss, namely that in which all factors of production are increasing at a constant geometric rate per unit of time but no other change is occurring, this opinion may be said to have got itself embodied in a little equation the authorship of which is to be attributed jointly to Mr Harrod and Professor Domar.[1] Let y be output in any period, $r = \dfrac{\dfrac{dy}{dt}}{y}$ its geometric rate of growth, q the assumedly unchanging proportion of required capital to output per period. Then the required rate of creation of

---

[1] Though the basic algebra of the 'steadily progressive economy' had already been explored by Cassel (*Theory of Social Economy*, ch. 1, §6) and Pigou (*Economics of Stationary States*, Appendix I).

capital is $q\dfrac{dy}{dt}$, or qry; so the required rate of saving sy is also equal to qry; so s, the proportion of income that must be saved to keep this system in 'dynamic equilibrium', is equal[1] to qr.

And I think, too, as I have already said, that in this simple case most people would agree that for the preservation of monetary equilibrium what is prima facie required – remember we agreed not to put it higher than that – is that the Monetary Authority should cause or permit the stock of money to grow at the same rate r as the factors of production, thus keeping the price level unchanged.

There would not, I am afraid, be the same unanimity as to what is to happen in certain other cases to which we must next turn our attention.

Let us next suppose that output is steadily increasing, but that capital is growing faster than population; and let us concentrate on the simplest and extreme case in which capital is growing but population constant. What behaviour of total money income, and hence of the money supply, does monetary equilibrium require? The difficulty here is that since the relative marginal productivities of the two hired factors, labour and waiting, are being continuously altered, it is not consistent with what we will call 'real' equilibrium that their money rates of reward should both remain unchanged. Hence the concept of monetary equilibrium as the state of affairs which keeps entrepreneur profits normal in face of the fixity of the money rates of reward of all the hired factors is not entirely applicable.

A solution which suggests itself is that in each period the flow of total money income ought to be such as to permit entrepreneurs to pay an unchanged wage-bill, plus

---

[1] E.g. if the annual rate of output at any time is 1,000, its annual rate of growth 3 per cent, the stock of capital in existence at that time 4,000, then in order to maintain the system in equilibrium the proportion of income saved must be 12 per cent.

such an interest-bill as is called for in the light of the displacement of the relative marginal productivities of waiting and labour. For instance, if the 'elasticity of substitution' between the two is unity, i.e. if the proportions of total product imputable to them are unchanged, the interest-bill will also be unchanged, and the total flow of money income can be unchanged, and prices can be permitted to fall in proportion to the increase in output. But if, as we have seen that some have argued is likely, the 'real' effect of an increase in capital is to increase the relative share accruing to capital, then to implement this result smoothly the total flow of money income must rise somewhat, and prices fall less than in proportion to the increase in output.

There is still however the complication that *old* contracts for interest payment cannot be speedily readjusted, but conform to our original assumption of fixity, so that to obviate all entrepreneur losses the flow of money income would have in any period to be greater, and the fall in prices therefore less, than is suggested by the considerations I have just advanced. It may be that some compromise policy is indicated, and that *any* compromise will have awkward differential effects as between different entrepreneurs. These difficulties are really inherent in the whole system of long-term contract, and are not removable by *any* monetary policy. Nevertheless the main point is, I think, clear, that if capital is growing while population is not, in some circumstances at least it is reasonable that the flow of total money income should increase – i.e. one need not and should not take the view, which has been put forward by some Austrian writers, that in all circumstances it is *money income per head* that the Authorities should seek to stabilise.

Now let us consider another kind of steady progress – not a growth in the *quantity* of any of the factors of production, but an increase of *x* per cent per unit of time in the *productivity* of each of them, owing to improvements in technique or organisation. What monetary policy does the preservation of equilibrium require?

At first sight the case seems to resemble closely that of a growth of the factors, – each man in any period is virtually becoming $\left(1 + \dfrac{x}{100}\right)$ men. But reflection shows that from the monetary standpoint there is, or may be, a great difference. Let us remind ourselves that in a closed system the main reason for pursuing one monetary policy rather than another is that the rewards per unit of time of the hired factors are sticky in terms of money: if it were not so, if the prices of all goods and services responded instantaneously and equally to alterations in the money stream, the size of that stream would be a matter of indifference. Hence it would seem that if the size of the money stream is expanded *pari passu* with the increase in productivity, while the rates of money wages, etc., remain fixed, there will accrue a windfall profit to entrepreneurs with disequilibrating results. To avoid this result, the money stream must be kept fixed in spite of the increase in productivity, and prices consequently be allowed to fall. True there will occur a consequent rise in the commodity value of all stocks of money, e.g. bank balances, held by individuals; but that will be a mere registration or reflection of the increase in productivity and will not imply a spontaneous act of thrift requiring to be utilised by an expansion of bank loans.

Conversely if for any reason productivity is decreasing (e.g. in an agricultural country as a result of bad harvests), prices should be allowed to rise, otherwise entrepreneurs will suffer windfall losses.

That is the argument for attempting to stabilise not the price-level of commodities but the price of productive power, i.e. for permitting a slow secular fall of prices in a community which is making technical progress. It is a strong argument, and one whose strength is generally admitted in regard to individual commodities and only disputed when the argument is generalised; e.g. nobody was surprised at the fall in the price of motor cars between 1900 and 1939 or supposed that it meant that car manufacturers were all along on the point of being driven out of business. Nevertheless, as usual, our final decision must be based on a weighing up of conflicting considerations. In particular it may be urged that the argument must be modified so far as the increase in productivity is accompanied by an automatic increase in hourly money rates of reward, as is apt to happen where systems of payment by result are in force. For piece-rates, etc., are sometimes hard to readjust downwards to take account of increasing productivity; so that to keep the aggregate money income stream constant would inflict windfall losses on many entrepreneurs.

The position of the *merchant* in a régime of steadily falling prices has also occasioned special anxiety. It seems at first sight that if he is always selling goods for less than he gave for them, then, even though he is able continuously to replace his stock at the lower level of prices, he must be making a series of capital losses, measured in money or in command over productive power, which, especially if he is operating on borrowed money, cannot but discourage him from continuing in business. Hawtrey, who is an advocate of letting prices fall in proportion to increases in productivity, says that this succession of realised losses will not affect the merchant's future behaviour as would a prospective fall in prices caused by a threatened contraction in money demand ('Money and Index-numbers', in *Art of Central Banking*, p. 324). But this does not seem a good enough reply if we are contemplating a definite and public policy of letting prices fall as productivity improves; for it will then always be

expected that productivity will improve and prices therefore fall, and new losses of the same kind therefore be
incurred by displaying enterprise.

The answer seems to be rather that we must assume
with regard to the merchant, as indeed we do with regard
to the producer himself, that the fall in price does not
occur till the end of the relevant part of the period of
process – which, it will be remembered, includes a normal
period of holding in stock – during which the increase in
productivity occurs. In other words there will be a normal
lag in the fall of retail behind the fall in wholesale prices
which will prevent the emergence for the merchant of the
capital loss so far assumed. It is only if he is holding
abnormally *old* stocks that he will suffer a capital loss on
them.

Nevertheless these various difficulties are sufficiently
real to make it desirable to avoid undue dogmatism as to
how, from the point of view of maintaining the incentives
to activity, the level of prices should be made to behave
when productivity is increasing. My own bias, like
Marshall's and Hawtrey's, is on the side of emphasising
the benefits of falling prices and the dangers of what I
should describe as pseudo-stabilisation: but I am somewhat more tolerant than I used to be of the other point of
view! And the issue still remains debatable when considerations of social justice and expediency are brought
into account. Prima facie there is much to be said for
Hawtrey's view (ibid., p. 317) that the real income of the
rentier – the widow, the unmarried daughter, the artist
son for whom an earner has attempted to make suitable
provision – as well as that of the pensioner and the non-
industrial worker – the don or M.P. – should be allowed
to increase *pari passu* with that of the industrial worker.
But no doubt some will maintain the opposite point of
view that, in the case at any rate of the rentier, the 'temper
of the age' demands an eating into his real income, if not

the compassing of his euthanasia. As regards the industrial worker, everybody agrees that his real income should increase if his productivity is increasing; but the price-stabiliser maintains, while others would question, that working-class psychology demands that the increase should occur through a continuous upward trend in the level of money wages. I suspect myself that there is some confusion here between what the individual desires to see happening to himself during his working life – naturally he attaches importance to securing 'rises' at reasonable intervals – and what a class insists on for its members of given age or experience. I suspect too that differences of sex psychology are involved, the earning man being prone to be more interested in the amount of money received, the shopping woman in what it will buy.

It must be remembered too that productivity is apt to increase at very different rates in different occupations. Hence if money wages are allowed to rise, at the point at which an increase in productivity has occurred, by the full amount of that increase in productivity, the rise is apt to spread to other occupations in which productivity has increased less or not at all, the spread occurring partly through the route of demand and partly through emulative wage claims aimed at preserving existing relativities in the reward for effort. The result of course is a rise in *average* wages in excess of the rise in *average* productivity, which on any reckoning is a departure from 'monetary equilibrium'.

Some pronouncements of British Government policy have been somewhat ambiguous in this matter, and there has undoubtedly been some tendency for the fruits of hoped-for increases in productivity to be promised away in advance twice over, – once in the form of rising wages and once in the form of falling cost of living, – not to mention a third and fourth time in the forms of extended social services and shorter hours. I suppose I must concede that the huge growth of national debts as a proportion of national income on the one hand, and the fear of Communist overbidding on the other, render it unlikely that, in present circumstances, a price-level falling in full proportion to increases in productivity will be unequivocally adopted in western countries as an objective of policy. And while in my heart I still hanker after that – the ideal Marshall-Hawtrey – policy, I shall be pretty well content if fifty years hence I look round and find the price-level no higher than it is today!

I must now bring this part of my argument to an end by reminding you that what I have been discussing is what policies, in the narrower or tactical sense, are called for under various conditions in order to preserve monetary equilibrium. I have tried not to take it for granted that the preservation of monetary equilibrium should be in all circumstances the overriding objective of policy in the wider or strategic sense. Indeed my little book on *Banking Policy and the Price Level* was written thirty years ago partly in order to suggest the contrary. Looking back on the history of capitalism, I should myself find it difficult to say dogmatically that such episodes as the English railway mania of the 1840s, or the American railway boom of 1869–71, or the German electrical boom of the 1890s, each of which drenched the country in question with valuable capital equipment at the expense of inflicting inflationary levies and adding to the instability of employment, were on balance 'a bad thing'. And in these more enlightened days if a community, even though making modest but steady progress, feels itself under an urgent need to equip itself rapidly with fixed capital instruments for purposes of defence, or for reaping the harvest of technical improvements in which it has for some reason lagged behind the rest of the world, the fact that a certain policy will involve monetary un-neutrality or disequilibrium cannot in my view be taken to be a decisive argument against it. As I suggested last term, we are far from being able to say that the amount of provision for the future which will be made by a free enterprise economy which preserves monetary equilibrium is in any absolute sense the 'right' amount. Thus the sort of analysis I have been conducting does not enable us to condemn off-hand Russian five-year plans, or Indian five-year plans, or any other nation's x- or y-year plans on the ground that they are inflationary. But it does perhaps direct a salutary light first on to the immediate cost in human welfare involved in such operations, and secondly on to the risk – again I would not presume to say the certainty, but the risk – that if pressed too far such policies will sow the seeds of their own breakdown by putting on the necks of the economic subjects a heavier yoke than they have consciously consented to bear – in the end, if there is any freedom left at all, some little voice will be heard to squeak 'Are these hardships really necessary?' and the rot will spread and the whole edifice come crashing to the ground. Even in totalitarian countries we have seen some dramatic instances in recent times of the evil consequences of pressing too far a policy of 'forced levying' in the interests of rapid capital accumulation. And for western countries at least, unless perhaps under the imminent threat of catastrophic war, I would now hold the pursuit of monetary equilibrium to be a sufficiently ambitious, and the wiser, path.

III

BANKING AND MONETARY EQUILIBRIUM

We have been discussing the criteria of, and the requisites for, monetary equilibrium. We must now go on to discuss the obstacles to its preservation, supposing that to be the object of policy. I should say myself that historically far the most important of these has been war, tending to promote disequilibrium in an upward or 'inflationary' direction. But we live in an age in which, though its best friend could not describe it as having been free from war, more attention has been concentrated on the obstacles tending to produce disequilibrium in the opposite or 'deflationary' direction. There need be no doubt that in progressive societies which have already attained, as judged by the standards of past history, a high level of wealth per head, such obstacles exist. But there is room for much debate as to how far they depend on certain fairly definite institutional features of modern free enterprise economies and how far on deeper and more pervasive forces; and again, so far as the latter is true, whether these forces are recurrent and epidemic or whether they are persistent and endemic – the issue which I have discussed briefly in my essay, 'The Snake and the Worm' – the snake of cyclical fluctuation and the worm of chronic stagnation.

Let us begin with certain institutional problems, the most important of which gives me occasion for saying all that I have time to say about a large and complicated subject – the theory and history of Banking. In modern free enterprise economies in peace-time, monetary policy, so far as it has been consciously pursued at all, has hitherto been mainly pursued through the agency of a system of private banks, subjected, with increasing frequency and closeness in recent decades, to the supervision and influence of a Central Bank. Now these banks have certain preferences as regards the nature of their assets. Traditionally, in Anglo-Saxon countries at least, the banks have regarded it as their main function to make advances for the building up of working capital.

Let us go back to what we learnt last term about the nature of working capital; and let us start with a stationary state. We saw that in such a state there would be in existence a mass of working capital, of goods in process of production or in store, equal to a certain proportion n, in the simple case one-half, of the output DR during a period of process D, where R stands for annual output and D is reckoned as a fraction of a year. Thus we got the equation $C=nDR$. Now, to fix our ideas by taking extreme cases, let us suppose that the whole of C has been built up in the past with the aid of the banks, and that the banks have not used any of their powers of money-creation for any other purpose. It does not matter in principle whether the owners of working capital are replenishing it daily out of the proceeds of their sales, or whether, as is nearer to real life and not inconsistent with our idea of stationariness, some of them are continually repaying loans to the banks and others borrowing, in accordance with seasonal needs, individual changes of fortune and so forth. We will suppose further that the only kind of money in circulation consists of balances with the banks; and that consequently the banks do not need to keep any kind of reserves.

What does this state of affairs imply? The real value of the money in the hands of the public is, as we know, $\dfrac{M}{P}=KR$, where K is the proportion of annual output over which the public wishes to keep command in the form of money, or, which comes to the same thing, the fraction of a year during which, on the average, a piece of money changes hands once in purchase of output. The real value of bank assets is $C=nDR$. Therefore, since the banks' balance-sheets balance, $KR=nDR$, or $K=nD$. Thus under the assumed conditions this relation between two different periods of time, the period of circulation of money against output and the period of process, is an underlying condition of equilibrium. Now there may, it is true, be *some* relation between the K of business firms and the length of the productive process; but in the main these two periods K and D are determined by different sets of psychological and technical conditions; and that one should be exactly $\frac{1}{2}$, or in the general case n times, the other could only be regarded as a fortunate accident.

Now let us relax the conditions a little in the direction of real life. Let us suppose that (1) the banks have created *some* money for other purposes than the building up of working capital: call a the proportion of their assets which *is* represented by working capital; (2) *some* working capital has been built up by entrepreneurs out of their own savings or by recourse to the general public: call b the proportion of working capital which has been built up by the aid of the banks. Thus only a proportion a of the whole money supply is 'backed by' working capital, and the working capital by which it is backed is only a proportion b of the whole working capital; and our condition for equilibrium becomes $aK=bnD$, or $K=\dfrac{b}{a}nD$.

Consider the implications of the equation. Our 'stationary state' is not lifeless — new individuals replace old, some firms are at any time repaying loans and others borrowing. If now, b being less than 1, some bright young entrepreneur tries, and tries successfully, to *make* it 1 in his case, i.e. to borrow the equivalent of the whole of his working capital from the banks, he will upset the apple-cart. The stream of money income will be increased out of proportion to the stream of final output, prices will rise, and what we have described as a 'forced levy' be inflicted on all spenders of income. Of course, the extra money will land up in somebody's balances ('saving will equal investment'), but that does not alter the fact that 'abstinence' has been inflicted, by its expenditure, on other people, or even by the bright young entrepreneurs, if there are many of them, mutually on themselves. This result will only be prevented if the banks take active steps to neutralise the increase in b by an increase in a, i.e. by a decline in the proportion of their non-working-capital assets. This they might effect if they could induce the public to buy from them some of these other assets instead of spending the money on final output of some kind or another.

These fundamental truths were known to the pioneers of English monetary theory 150 years ago, especially to that remarkable man Henry Thornton, who in his *Paper Credit of Great Britain* (1802, reprinted 1939, p. 244) wrote of the 'error of imagining that a proper limitation of bank notes may be sufficiently secured by attending merely to the nature of the security for which they are given'. Nevertheless, when in the 1920s the new Federal Reserve Board got into the saddle in the United States as the arbiter of banking policy, and felt impelled to define the principles on which the new Federal Reserve Banks would lend to the member banks, it nailed its colours to the mast of the doctrine of 'productive credit'. Here are two sentences from its famous Report for the year 1923. 'The Federal Reserve system is a system of productive credit. It is not a system of credit for either investment or speculative purposes.' 'It is the belief of the Board that there is little danger that the credit created and distributed by the Federal Reserve Banks will be in excessive volume if restricted to productive uses.' And by a number of rulings which it gave about 'eligible paper', i.e. about the kinds of credit instrument which the member banks could bring to the Reserve Banks for re-discount, the Board showed that by 'productive uses' it meant the building up of working capital.

But before straying further into history, let me return to the pure theory of banking in the stationary state. Suppose that, while it remains stationary in respect of population and fixed capital, there occurs, as a result of technical change, a reduction in D, or, as a result of change in personal or business habits, a reduction in b or an increase in K. Then it is evident that a tendency to disequilibrium will be set up in the opposite direction to that which I was describing just now – namely in the direction of a wastage of thrift, a conferment of 'anti-levies' or uncovenanted consumption on some members of the public, and a discouragement to output and employment. This situation could only be redressed if the banks were prepared to depart more extensively from the doctrine of productive credit – in terms of the equation to reduce a. And if we are to adhere to the assumption of stationariness, so that the creation of additional fixed capital is ruled out, this could presumably only mean the dishing out of money, in some guise or other, for the purpose of financing *consumption*.

Now let us ask what happens to our formula for the attainment of banking equilibrium, $K = \dfrac{b}{a} nD$, in a growing economy.[1] The attempt to answer this question led into some algebra in which, with expert help, I tried at one time to dabble about. Briefly, it appeared that for a con-

---

[1] This paragraph reproduces pretty exactly what I have been in the habit of saying. But Mr. A. D. Roy, who has again kindly come to my assistance, warns me that in his opinion the special assumptions which I have made yield only a very rough approximation to the complex truth. I must warn the reader accordingly that the whole paragraph is suspect. But the general conclusion that, even in theory, the appropriate banking policy for a growing community is a pretty tricky business is, I think, reinforced. (D.H.R. 1958.)

stant *arithmetic* rate of growth the formula stands; but that for a constant *geometric* rate of growth by a fraction x per period of process, while K can still bear a constant ratio[1] to $\frac{b}{a}nD$, that ratio must be greater than in a stationary economy. *How much* greater depends on the lag which we suppose to be required for each new batch of population, including of course firms as well as individuals, to build up money balances on the representative scale. If for simplicity we make the arbitrary assumption that each new batch builds up *no* new balances in the period of process in which it is first drawn into employment, but builds up the *whole* of its required balances in the next succeeding period of process, then the formula[2] becomes $K=\frac{b}{a}nD(1+x)$. If the lag is greater than this, K – the hoarding propensity of the public – must be greater if the occurrence of inflationary disequilibrium is to be prevented.

There is perhaps not much to be gained by pursuing such subtleties further; but they suggest, I think, two reflections. First, even in a relatively stable society which has not become prey to fluctuations, the management of the money income stream would be likely to be a pretty empirical business, working by trial and error and not able to count on hitting the theoretical mark with great precision. Secondly, the fact that things went as well as they did in the period 1815–1914, which it is convenien: to call the nineteenth century, seems to have been partly

[1] The condition for constancy seems to be that the *increment* of population per period of process should grow at a constant proportionate rate. This condition is fulfilled both by a constant arithmetic and by a constant geometric rate of the growth of population.

[2] As I have suggested (*Economic Commentaries*, No. IV) this formula has affinities with the Harrod-Domar formula, (see p. 37 above). its differential feature (which is my excuse for inflicting it on you!) being that it tries to take account of the particular phenomenon of banking preferences.

due to a happy accident, namely to a fortunate but precarious harmony between the desire of people to entrust real resources to the keeping of the banks and the desire of entrepreneurs to borrow for working capital purposes. Later this harmony seems to have been progressively undermined by certain secular changes – more marked in the United States but extending also to this country. The period of process tended to contract owing to the speeding up of transport and communications, reinforced in the United States in the 1920s by a definite campaign for the simplification of products and the reduction of inventories. Again, with the growth of firms business became more capable of looking after its own needs for working capital; such concerns as United Steel and Ford's, the Macmillan Committee were told twenty-five years ago, never borrowed from their banks; and when a big firm took over a small one the first thing it did was to pay off the latter's overdraft. Thus in terms of our equation b and D both declined. Further, though this can't be shown in our simplified equation, the banks came to attract a greater share of the hoarding propensities of the public, commercial bank balances competing successively, as stores of value, with coins and notes on the one hand and with savings bank deposits on the other.

The banks had to react by finding means to reduce a, i.e. to expand the range of their assets: but in doing so they were hampered, naturally enough, by their preoccupation with the need for 'liquidity', which has prevented them from taking a very active part in the formation of fixed capital. It is true that in both countries loans nominally made for short periods are often outstanding for much longer; and in the United States the strict doctrine of 'productive credit' never proved possible to enforce – it was too easy to discount 'eligible paper' with the Reserve Banks and use the proceeds for ineligible purposes – and was ultimately abandoned. In both countries, too, the banks have lent in connection with house-building. They have also lent, for use in the purchase of stock exchange securities, money some, though not all, of which percolates through fairly directly into the purchase of capital goods: but such activities have always been kept within narrow bounds in the United Kingdom, and, since 1929, in the United States as well, through well-grounded apprehension of repetition of the speculative excesses to which they have led in the past. Finally, some part of the large proportion of loans made by the British banks for 'personal and professional' purposes can doubtless be regarded as of a capital-forming nature.

But they have also turned increasingly, at any rate in the United States, to financing consumption; and above all, in both countries, to the holding of Government securities, which from their point of view are reasonably liquid in the sense that in case of need they can be shunted off – or so it is the convention to believe – without great loss on to other people, though of course from the social point of view the thrift embodied in them, having mostly been shot off into the air at various dates, is far more 'illiquid', i.e. undisentangleable, than that embodied in a factory or a machine. And superimposed on the secular trends of which I have been speaking have come two great wars and a great slump, the wars leading in both countries and the slump in the United States to vast issues of new Government securities to finance current expenditure, and giving the banks a full job of work to do in canalising for the use of Government any thrift which might otherwise have been in danger of going to waste. The resulting changes in the composition of bank assets are illustrated in the tables on p. 57; and in interpreting the British one it must be remembered that even the short-term assets are now mainly devoted to the finance of Government, the bills being mostly Treasury Bills and the short loans to the discount market mostly employed in carrying various forms of Government paper.

These events have assisted the banks in postponing their secular problem; further, one feature of the post-war boom, the difficulty which firms have been under in financing stock replacements and maintenance of fixed capital out of heavily taxed profits when prices are rising has tended to send industry back to their doors. Indeed, as everybody knows, the particular problem in 1955–7 has been to prevent the volume of bank advances from rising too fast. But the secular problem may some day reassert itself, and some of the bankers have shown awareness of its existence. Lord Wardington of Lloyds Bank, in his last chairman's speech (1945), spoke of their 'intention of being more elastic in our view of what constitutes a legitimate business loan' and of instructions having been given to the advances department accordingly. You will have been told, too, *ad nauseam* of the two semi-public corporations, the I.C.F.C., with its capital of £15 millions and borrowing powers of £30 millions to provide permanent capital for small firms, to be financed entirely by the banks, and the larger F.C.I. with capital of £25 millions provided by an outside consortium so strong and respectable that the banks should have no hesitation in lending the £100 millions it is authorised to borrow: though it should be noticed that support of these bodies to the full legal limit would only employ some 2 per cent of the banks' deposits. More recently some of the banks have joined a consortium for financing the construction of tankers. In the United States there have been more definite signs, for good or evil, of a forward policy, the so-called 'term loan', sometimes made for as much as ten years, having had a considerable vogue since the war, and constituting now about a third of all commercial loans.

On the whole subject, please see my little essay called

'Is there a future for banking?'[1] – also, if you can get hold
of it, an important address by Sir George Erskine (of
Morgan Grenfell) to the Institute of Bankers on May 18,
1955. It was not well received by the commercial
bankers, and was not perhaps very happily timed, since
bank advances were at that moment increasing with
embarrassing speed! Indeed, as part of the general dis-
inflationary policy, it has been felt necessary in quite
recent years to subject bank lending for fixed capital
purposes to special supervision and discouragement by
the Capital Issues Committee. But I suspect that from a
longer-run point of view Erskine may have had hold of
the right end of the stick.

There I must leave the banks, and allude more briefly
to two other modern developments of the free enterprise
system which, it has been argued, may hinder the preservation of monetary equilibrium. One is somewhat similar
to the banking developments we have just examined,
namely the great growth of institutional savings made
through provident funds, insurance companies and the
like, instead of either being placed privately or offered on
an open capital market. The investment policy of such
bodies normally tends to be somewhat rigid and to seek
safety at all costs, with the result that a plethora of thrift
may appear in some sectors of the economy, while in
others investment opportunities remain unreaped. Many
of these institutions have realised this danger and revised
their investment policies accordingly; ordinary shares as
a percentage of total investments of members of the
British Insurance Association rose from 3·4 in 1927 and
10·6 in 1947 to 15·4 in 1955.[2] Indeed, one of the dangers
of a prolonged period of inflation is that the reaction will
be carried too far, and that, in their anxiety to find a hedge
against the depreciation of money, Pension Funds,

[1] No. 14 of the book *Utility and All That*.
[2] *The Banker*, September 1956, p. 579.

Colleges, Churches and similar bodies will be impelled to shoulder industrial risks to an extent which ill accords with their degree, while the Government will find it increasingly difficult to raise funds at fixed interest for its schemes of public investment. Thus, as in the case of banking, the immediate danger seems to be of precisely the opposite character to that which appeared to be materialising in the pre-war decades.

The other feature which has been questioned is the tendency of large joint stock companies, even though not, as in this country in some recent years, impelled by quasi-compulsory dividend limitation, to conserve their profits in their own business. If the profits are not spent, this may have a definite deflationary effect: but even if they are spent on equipment and so forth, the effect, it is argued, may be less generally stimulating than if they were distributed as dividends and so found their way into an open capital market where they would be available to be borrowed by new and growing firms who would make better use of them. I suspect myself that this is, from a long-run point of view, a real point – a needed corrective to enthusiasm over the 'ploughing back' of profits as an indisputably good thing, and a strong argument against permanent limitation of dividends. But I suspect that its relevance is to the problem of the efficient *distribution* of productive resources to meet consumer needs rather than to our present theme of the forces tending to cause productive resources to remain unused. And certainly in some recent years even the largest companies seem to have had good use for ploughed back profits in supplementing depreciation allowances which have proved inadequate, in face of rising prices, to keep real capital intact.

And now let me conclude my survey of these institutional problems of a modern capitalist society by saying dogmatically that I believe them to be real ones, not to be ignored and requiring ingenuity and public spirit for their solution, but soluble within the framework of a free enterprise society if there is a will to solve them, and not in themselves compelling the reduction of banks, insurance companies and large corporations to the status of functionless appendages of an all-controlling Governmental machine of investment.

(1) U.K. *Clearing Banks* (10 *in* 1929, 11 *since*)

	1929	1938	1945	1956
Gross deposits, £m.	1800	2277	4692	6288
		% of gross deposits		
Bills and short money... ...	21	19	8	27
T.D.R.'s	—	—	39	—
Investments	14	28	25	31
Advances, etc.	55	43	16	30

(2) U.K. *All Banks – Advances*

	Feb. 1946	Feb. 1957
Total, £m.	848	2000
	%c	%
Agriculture	8	11
Retail trade	7	8
Entertainment, religion, etc.	4	2
Metal trades	10	15
All other industry and trade	23	29
Local authorities	9	4
Public utilities (ex. transport)... ...	1	3
Financial	9	12*
Personal and professional	28	16

* Including hire purchase 1.

(3) U.S. *Member Banks*

	Mid 1929	Mid 1938	End 1945	Sept. 1956
Loans and investments, $M. ...	36	30½	107	136
	% of total loans and investments			
Loans on real estate	9	9	3	13
Loans for securities	} 62	} 33	6	3
Loans all other			12	40
Securities, U.S. Government...	12	40	73	34
„ other	17	18	6	10

(4) *U.S. Consumer Credit, $M.*

				End 1939	End 1945	End 1950	End 1956
Instalment	...	...	...	4·5	2·5	14·7	31·8
Total ...	...	...	...	7·2	5·7	21·4	42·1

IV

THE STAGNATION THESIS

It is, however, widely held that the difficulty of maintaining monetary equilibrium in a rich society depends not only on institutional features of the kind I have been discussing, but on a deep-seated tendency for the desire to save to be continually outrunning the opportunities for profitable investment. This is the doctrine which I alluded to last term as the 'stagnation thesis', and which is invested by its advocates with varying degrees of generality. Keynes, in most of his later work, gives the impression that he believes it to be relevant to the greater part of human history, with an honourable exception for the period of expansion which we loosely call the nineteenth century. Beveridge, with the usual tendency of the neophyte to go one better than the established priesthood, seems inclined to apply it to the nineteenth century as well. American writers are more apt to take the line that after preliminary symptoms in the 1920s – that queer period which I once ventured to describe as a sloom followed by a bump – the phenomenon in question first really became evident in the 1930s; but that since these inter-war experiences were bound up with certain irreversible events, notably the so-called 'disappearance of the frontier' – the filling up of the physical area of the North American continent – they can fairly be taken as a good guide to what is in store in the future, once the period of post-war reconstruction, which has gone on longer than anybody expected, is over.

What we have to do then is to look again at the stagnation thesis in its more distinctively monetary aspects. But we cannot do that effectively without bringing out

again on parade the queer beast whom I have so far
scarcely mentioned this term, though you have no doubt
noticed him lurking in the background, – our old friend
or enemy the rate of interest; so that it will be convenient
for me at this point to spend a little time in bringing
together some of what I have to say about the rate of
interest in its monetary aspects.

The first question which we have to face is this. Now
that we are explicitly taking account of monetary phenomena, is there any need for us to revise the common-
sense idea which we formed last term of what the rate of
interest *is* – namely that it is the price of the use of
investable funds, arrived at in the market, like other
prices, as the result of the interaction of schedules of
demand and supply? I feel convinced that there is not.
But of course we must now take account of the fact that
on the supply side of the market there are sometimes to be
found not merely the two things which figured in our
original formulation, namely (1) newly saved money and
(2) money being liberated by depreciation quotas, etc.,
from entanglement in capital goods; but also two additional things, namely (3) money being withdrawn from
store by individuals and (4) money being newly created
by banks. And on the demand side there is sometimes to
be found not merely a demand for funds, or if you like an
offer of bonds or securities of some kind or other in order
to obtain funds, to be used for productive purposes; but
also a demand for funds, or if you like an offer of securities
in order to obtain funds, to be put into store.

I think it is now generally agreed[1] that there is no
necessary conflict between this way of looking at the
matter and that which, to quote my own formulation
(*Essays*, p. 8), 'portrays the rate of interest as the child of

[1] Only Mrs Robinson, I think, still finds the concept of loanable or investable funds so
obscure as to compel her to perform prodigies of self-stigmatisation and expectoration.
See *The Accumulation of Capital*, pp. 402–3.

a marriage between the amount of money which the monetary authority permits to be in existence at [any] moment and a schedule exhibiting the amounts of money which, in the light of their knowledge of the existence of various rates of interest, people would wish to hold at that moment.' Keynes was, I feel sure, mistaken in supposing that the two methods were 'radically opposed'. Indeed the relation between them bears a certain analogy to that between the two forms of the price-level equation, the one containing Marshall's K and the one containing Fisher's V. And it can be argued that just as Marshall's version of price theory is more fundamental than Fisher's, so is Keynes's formulation of interest theory more fundamental than mine, because it fastens attention directly on the state of psychological preference. Nevertheless I am of opinion that Keynes's own handling of his apparatus illustrates the great dangers to which its use is exposed, unless constantly checked by reference to what is happening in the capital market. And it will be convenient if at this point I attempt to re-state my two main objections to Keynes's treatment – smoothing over at first the lesser of the two in order to concentrate attention on the greater.

In Keynes's treatment, you will remember, the stock of money held by the public consists of two parts – the active money held for the conduct of industry and trade and the idle money held for what are described as 'speculative purposes'. Without looking more closely for the moment into these 'speculative purposes', let us remind ourselves that it is the idle money which is directly linked up with the rate of interest, for the lower the rate which people could obtain by using it, the more money will they be disposed to hold idle. Or, putting the same truth another way round, the more money is chucked at them by the Monetary Authority to hold idle, the lower the rate of interest that can be established.

But the active money also comes into the story. Keynes's

treatment of it in his book is rather confusing, for the first time it is mentioned (p. 171) we are led to expect that we shall find a large volume of active money associated with a low rate of interest, since a low rate of interest stimulates capital outlay and capital outlay begets trade activity. But a good many pages later (p. 248) he reaches the orthodox, and I think correct, conclusion that a large volume of active money will normally be associated with a *high* rate of interest. This – in his language – is because, given the total supply of money which the Authority permits to exist, the more of it is active the less is available to satisfy the public's desire to keep money idle, and the higher, therefore, the rate of interest must be.

There are thus two possible causes tending to raise the rate of interest, the one an increase in economic activity, the other a movement of confidence of some kind leading people to desire to hold more money idle at any given rate of interest. We may compare the conclusion reached long ago by Marshall (*M.C.C.*, p. 254): 'The rate of interest often rises rather high, under the influence of hope, in an ascending phase of industrial and commercial activity and prosperity; but it seldom rises very high for that reason. On the other hand, it may be raised to a vast height by fears that commercial or political disturbances may soon restrict the operations of credit.'

Diagrammatically the point may be represented as follows: Measure money along OX, the rate of interest along OY. ON is the total quantity of money, of which OM is active and MN idle. LP is the curve connecting the amount of idle money which people wish to hold with the rate of interest. Then, given ON, the rate of interest may rise from NQ to NR *either* because (Fig. i), OM being increased to OM', LP is simply *displaced* to the right, becoming L'P', *or* because (Fig. ii), OM remaining unchanged, LP is *raised* throughout its length to become L'P'. In (i) an amount of 'speculative' money M'N'

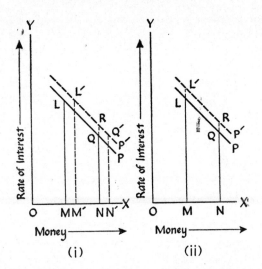

(i)   (ii)

$(= MN)$, if it were available, would still be associated with a rate of interest $N'Q'$ $(=NQ)$; in (ii) the same amount of 'speculative' money MN is associated with a higher rate of interest NR.

But having thus, though somewhat as an afterthought, distinguished the two separate causes which may raise the rate of interest – the *hope* cause and the *fear* cause, as Marshall calls them in the passage I have just quoted – Keynes shows no disposition to maintain the distinction between them for the purposes of clinical treatment. Whichever the reason for which the rate shows a tendency to elevate itself, it is to be knapped on the head, like the cockney's eels in *King Lear*, with a cry of 'Down, wanton, down'. Since the 'active money' cause contains wrapped up in itself – though, as I think, very inadequately expressed – all those forces of invention, development, population growth and so on which figure in neo-classical theory as tending to raise the rate of interest, this is evidently a very serious matter. The first occasion on which Keynes explicitly applied his doctrine to a concrete situation may be found recorded, by those who care to look up the files, in a little three-cornered brush between him, the then editor of the *Economist* and myself in the issues of that paper for February 6 and February 13, 1937. 'If the public is deprived of its normal supply of idle balances by the demand for active balances,' wrote Keynes, 'or if it gets nervous about the prospects of the gilt-edged market' – the two causes, you see, are put on exactly the same footing – then extra balances ought, he says, to be created for it by the Monetary Authority, and withdrawn later 'as a change in the atmosphere or the circumstances permits'. 'It is not easy,' he added, perhaps a little patronisingly, 'to get used to the idea of trying to avoid booms and slumps' – a remark which laid him open to the reply that it isn't made any easier by representing an inflammatory action as if it were a sedative one, and that in the words which I have quoted about withdrawing the excess balances when the situation alters, he was apparently, alone among economists, advocating the deliberate *contraction* of credit in a slump!

I have gone rather deeply into this matter because it is, I believe, the canker at the heart of the Keynesian theory of interest – a canker which has since (if cankers can so act) abundantly come home to roost, both in this country and in the United States. There are doubtless many reasons, fiscal and political, which account for the attempts made in both countries since the war to maintain and intensify 'cheap money' in the face of inflation. But a large share of responsibility must, I think, be attributed to the trick of what is now called semantics by which a magic phrase – liquidity preference – which had originally been chosen to denote one thing was quietly extended to cover also another thing with quite different economic implications.

I turn to the second of my main objections to Keynes's treatment. In what I have just said I have taken for granted the validity of his schedule connecting the desire to hold idle money with the rate of interest. But this needs further looking into. In his classification, the money held for what he calls 'precautionary' purposes, i.e. because of general uncertainty about what is going to happen, is included, rather unexpectedly, in 'active' money, the only 'idle' money being that which is held for what he calls 'speculative' purposes, i.e. which is being held off the gilt-edged market because it is thought that the price of gilt-edged securities will some day be lower than it is now. It is only with this part of the stock of money – a part which under stable conditions would not exist at all – that in his main argument, at least, he brings the rate of interest into direct touch. For the theory to operate, there must be a number of wealthy and acute people who, if the rate goes down, will expect with various degrees of conviction that it will sooner or later go up again to its 'normal' level and that their bonds will depreciate on their hands, and who therefore seek to hold money instead.

Now the trouble about this theory is that while it tells us something about what determines the divergence between the actual and the normal rates, it tells us nothing whatever about what determines the normal rate and therefore, given the degree of divergence, the actual rate. We cannot, consistently with this theory, describe the actual rate, as Keynes himself at moments seems inclined to do, as measuring the cost of the uncertainty or risk involved in holding bonds rather than money; for if there were no uncertainty at all, i.e. if the rate were expected with complete confidence to go back to normal after a certain interval, the actual rate would not vanish to zero, but would simply stand at a certain definite level below the normal rate.

The matter can be put quite precisely, on certain sim-

E

plifying assumptions, as follows. Let $p=$the normal, $x=$the actual rate, each expressed as a fraction. Then the present price of a perpetual £1 bond bearing interest p is $\frac{p}{x}$ instead of being 1. Let the rate be expected to remain at x for n years and then return by one jump to p. Neglecting compound interest, if I buy such a bond and hold it for n years, saving the interest, I shall, at the end of that time, possess $np + 1$. If I hold the purchase price in money I shall have $\frac{p}{x}$. In equilibrium the attractions of pursuing these alternative courses must be equal, i.e.:

$$np + 1 = \frac{p}{x}, \text{ or } x = \frac{p}{np + 1}. \text{ E.g. if } p = \frac{1}{20}, n = 5, \text{ then } x = \frac{1}{25}.$$

But all this tells us nothing as to why p isn't, say, $\frac{1}{5}$ instead of $\frac{1}{20}$, and x therefore, in accordance with the formula, $\frac{1}{10}$ instead of $\frac{1}{25}$.[1]

Thus Keynes's so-called 'speculative' theory turns out not to be really a theory of interest at all, but only a theory of the influences limiting speculative movements in the rate. It does not, of course, follow that it is not, provided we realise its ancillary nature, an interesting and important contributory element to the whole picture. Furthermore, Keynes's so-called speculative motive is not the sole channel for monetary influences on the rate of interest. As I have pointed out in my *Essays*, the older Cambridge writers, Lavington and Pigou, were in a sense kinder to 'liquidity preference', naturally interpreted, than Keynes

---

[1] Our result $x = \frac{p}{np+1}$ can be written $p = \frac{x}{1-nx}$, which if x is small is approximately $= x(1+nx) = x + nx^2$. Thus our formula, apart from neglecting compound interest (which of course we need not do) is approximately equivalent to that implicit in Keynes's statement (*General Theory*, p. 202) that the position of indifference for the investor is that in which the rate of interest is expected to rise annually, over the period foreseen, by the square of itself.

himself. For they were concerned, as he was not, to set in a functional relation with the rate of interest the money held for 'precautionary' purposes, because people do not know what is going to happen, because they are afraid that debts owing to them may not be paid at the due date, because (as Marshall emphasises) they might otherwise miss a sudden chance of making an advantageous bargain. It is true that in their formulation the rate appears as itself determined by outside forces and as in its turn affecting K, the desire to hold resources in monetary form, K in its turn, together with M, determining not the rate of interest but the price-level. And that, as I have said, I believe to be a pretty good formulation of the long-run truth. But that need not, and should not, prevent us from representing changes in the quantity of money, and in the desire to hold resources in monetary form, as exercising a short-run reciprocal influence on the rate of interest; and in my formulation of the 'investable funds' approach I have explicitly done so. But we must remember that such changes may also directly affect other prices as well. Bonds are not the only alternative to money as a use for resources, even for the private person, still less for the entrepreneur; and a theory of money which insists on working everything through the bond market – a College Bursars' theory, as it has been called – seems to me lacking in realism and comprehensiveness.

We are now ready to return to the stagnation thesis, and to examine the account which has been given by its advocates of the damaging effect, in a progressive economy, of an increase in the desire to save. Suppose that in a society in which there is already some saving I decide to save more, for instance to save an additional £100 out of my income instead of, as hitherto, spending it on beautiful clothes. There is no dispute now (though it was not always realised in the past) that if my saving simply takes the form of allowing my bank balance to increase, that will normally retard the circulation of money and depress the general level of money income and trade activity.[1] The case over which controversy has arisen is that in which I spend the saved money on a purchase of securities: so let us try to follow it out. My action destroys £100 of the income of my tailor and his workpeople and depletes their balances by £100. As against this, however, according to 'classical' theory, if you like to call it so, my £100 will, under any normal conditions, work its way through the capital market to create new income and money balances for builders, engineers, etc., equal to those which it has destroyed for the tailors, and, subject to minor frictions, the general level of income and activity will remain unchanged. For while the security which I buy is probably an old security, not a new issue, my action in buying it helps to create ease and buoyancy in the capital market; the professional dealers who compose that market can be relied upon to pass on in due course into the hands of entrepreneurs any money which they receive from the outside public; and in giving a simplified account of what happens we need not bother about the inner mechanics of the market for securities any more than we normally bother about the inner mechanics of the commodity markets in tracing the effect, on the total incomes of producers of consumable goods, of switches in the flow of money from purchasing one kind of consumable good to purchasing another.

In the writings of Keynes and his expositors challenging this optimistic conclusion there are, I think, to be found two separate lines of thought, one of which directs our attention in a barren, the other in a fruitful, direction. According to the first, my act of thrift will produce *no* easing of the situation in the capital market and hence *no*

---

[1] An exception to this is that if the money is definitely transferred from current to deposit account, and if the country is one in which (as in the U.S.A.) the banks keep a lower ratio of reserves to deposit than to current accounts, my action may enable my bank to expand its loans or investments and so to counteract my act of hoarding.

increase of activity in the instrumental trades, since my 'saving' is balanced by an equal and opposite 'dissaving' on the part of other people. Sometimes this is just asserted without argument, as by Mrs Robinson on p. 14 of her 'Introduction'. But sometimes the argument is developed in an at first sight rather plausible form. A loss-making entrepreneur – the tailor in my story – will, it is argued, sell securities in order to 'meet' or 'cover' his losses, and will thereby impose a burden on the capital market equal to that which is being taken off it by the saver. Now if the tailor is really determined to maintain both his personal consumption and his business activity intact by drawing on his capital in this way, it is true that all my savings will be swallowed up in keeping him afloat; but it is also true that so long as he persists in behaving in this manner there is no condition of trade depression or unemployment requiring correction through a stimulus to activity in the instrumental trades. Thus this argument depends for its validity on the assumption that in the face of entrepreneur losses full employment will always be maintained; evidently therefore it is not very effective as an explanation of the causation of *un*employment. It seems evident that this is an unstable situation which cannot continue, and that we shall not reach a solution along these lines.

I turn therefore to the other, more fruitful, line of thought, which brings us back to our old friend 'liquidity preference'. The effect of the first impact of my £100 on the securities market is to raise slightly the price of bonds, i.e. to lower slightly the rate of interest. At this lower rate of interest some people – either the professional dealers who compose the market or outside persons – will prefer to hold money rather than bonds. Thus the fall in the rate of interest is checked, and in effect part of my saved £100 is waylaid in inactive balances and does not work its way through on to the markets for instrumental goods. The net result, then, is some fall in the rate of interest and some increase in capital outlay, but a net decrease in the total flow of money income and (having regard to the stickiness of factor prices) probably in employment and output.

So put, and on the assumption that for one reason or another the desire of people to hold resources in the form of money is to a significant extent a function of the rate of interest, this argument seems to me perfectly sound. To its quantitative significance from a long-run point of view I will return presently. Meanwhile let me dwell for a moment on two points of language. (1) Keynes and his expositors are very insistent that in such a situation the increase of thrift only operates to lower the rate of interest *through* lowering total income. I should say rather that it also, and primarily, operates quite directly to lower the rate of interest by increasing the demand for securities, and that this fall in the rate of interest, by leading to an increase in K, leads also to a decline in the total income stream, i.e. prevents the income of builders and engineers from rising as much as the income of tailors has fallen. (2) Be it observed that what has happened can be expressed perfectly well in terms of the symbol K or of its convenient verbal equivalent 'hoarding', defined as taking steps to increase the existing proportion of one's money stock to one's money income. But the hoarding in this case has not been performed by the saver himself, as it would have been if he had saved simply by not drawing a cheque for £100 in favour of his tailor, i.e. if his savings had taken the form of an increase in his bank balance. The hoarding has been done by those persons, whoever they may be, who have been tempted by the fall in the rate of interest to increase their holdings of money.

Now to return to the point of substance. Who are the people who operate this liquidity trap, and how important is their action likely to be from a long-run point of view? Let us look again at the curve connecting the desire to hold money with the rate of interest, only getting rid of one complication by measuring now along OX not units of money but units of real resources over which command is to be held in monetary form, so that the curve comes to bear a close family resemblance to that which I used in expounding the Cambridge monetary equation, except that we are now measuring along OY not units of utility but rates of interest. If this curve is very elastic, newly saved money will be readily mopped up in the liquidity trap in response to a very small fall in the rate of interest: in the extreme case when it is horizontal, *but in that case only*, an increase in the desire to save will have *no* effect in reducing the rate of interest.

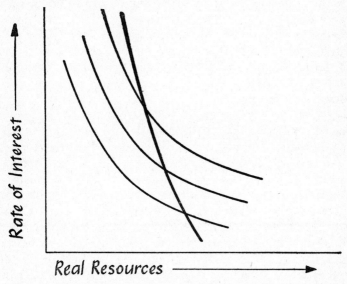

Let me first call attention to one great obstacle which Keynes himself put in the way of understanding his doctrine on this matter. All the undertones of his book, with its emphasis on the ineffectiveness of thrift in promoting investment, lead one to suppose that he is treating the curve as being perfectly elastic. Lange, for instance (listed article, pp. 177 and 190) explicitly says that this is Keynes's view, and Keynes commended Lange's article as having 'followed very closely and accurately his line of thought'. Yet in his book Keynes nowhere says that he is treating the curve as being infinitely elastic, and in one place (p. 207) definitely states the contrary; for he then says that while the limiting case where liquidity preference may become virtually absolute might become practically important in future, he knows of no example of it hitherto. All this makes it very difficult to be sure just what is being asserted.

Anyway we must endeavour to form our own opinion on the long-run elasticity of the curve; and in doing so it is necessary to distinguish between Keynes's own interpretation of 'liquidity preference' in terms of his 'speculative motive', and that broader interpretation, in terms of desire for protection against the general uncertainties of business life, which I have attributed to certain pre-Keynesian writers.

As regards the former, we have seen that while Keynes's theory offers an explanation of the divergence of x, the rate prevailing at any moment of time, from p the normal rate, it offers no explanation of the level of p, the normal rate itself. What this seems to point to is that p must be determined by people's estimate of the pressure of outside forces of some kind; and it seems natural to suggest that in a free enterprise economy these forces are none other than our old friends productivity and thrift. If this be so, then, in the absence of sufficient counter-pressure from invention or population growth, this expected rate p is likely to shift continually downwards as, in consequence of a successful process of capital accumulation, the marginal productivity of invested resources declines; and in that case the short-run speculative liquidity curve will shift downwards bodily with it. The path connecting the successive points of equilibrium reached on these transitory curves will look something like a vertical line. Thus we seem to be back to something very like the classical theory.

Now let us look at those broader 'precautionary' motives for holding money idle which, as we have seen, must also be regarded as in some measure sensitive to the counterpull of the prospect of earning a rate of return, whether by investment in real assets or in securities. Here the long-run truth is harder to discern, for evidently we have to do with motives which are stabler, more independent and less derivative, than the expectational motive on which Keynes himself lays stress. Nevertheless (though I feel less clear about this than about what I have said so far), here too it does not seem to me essential to suppose that the annual flow of advantage derived from holding the nth unit of resources in the form of money will in all circumstances be evaluated as equivalent to the same annual flow of product, whatever annual flow of product is obtainable by investing a unit of resources in real things. Rather, I suggest, one must suppose that it will be revised downwards as the yield obtainable from real investment becomes established at a lower level. If this be true, then even the short period curves of liquidity preference proper, like Keynes's short period curves of speculative pseudo-liquidity preference, seem to be really a sort of emanation from the fundamental curve of marginal productivity of investable funds rather than independent entities. A line joining the successive points of temporary equilibrium reached in them will, if not actually vertical, display a much smaller degree of elasticity than the curves themselves. In any case, it ought not to be beyond the capacity of a Monetary Authority to deal with a *steady* increase of this kind in K, i.e. to dish out enough money to keep money income per head constant, or increasing at an appropriate rate, in face of it.

The conclusion to which all this seems to lead is that the existence of the liquidity trap is much less likely than it has lately been fashionable to suppose to present a formidable long-run obstacle to the percolation of saved money through the capital markets into productive investment. And as regards the cyclical fluctuations to which we shall come in due course, it is, I think,[1] far rather the *variability* of K – the propensity to hoard, or whatever we like to call it – than its alleged elasticity to the rate of interest that should command our attention. Nevertheless I would agree that we ought not to exclude from our theoretical purview the case which Pigou has described as Keynes's Day of Judgment. This is the case in which the forces of productivity and thrift have so worked as to permit the rate of interest to fall to zero, or perhaps to some positive level a little above zero. What is to happen then? Marshall several times (*Principles*, pp. 232, 582) permits himself to play with the idea that the rate of interest might become negative. But it would seem that so long as it is possible to hold money at no cost that could never happen; for it would always be more advantageous to hold money than to accept a negative rate of return on real investment. If in such conditions the desire to save still continued unchecked, then we *should* get a progressive shrinkage in the stream of money income which it would be very difficult for the Monetary Authority to counteract. Whether this would necessarily involve massive *unemployment* is a question we can return to more conveniently in a later connection; but it would certainly be a very uncomfortable world to live in. You will no doubt recall, even if you were not convinced by, the case I presented last term for supposing that the arrival of the Day of Judgment would be prevented by the strong inducement to decumulate capital which would come into force – I am

---

[1] In this agreeing with Fellner, for a summary of whose view see Haley in *Survey of Contemporary Economics*, p. 44.

inclined to say which did in the 1940s show strong signs of coming into force – at very low levels of interest, and which would inhibit any further fall.

It is time for some closing remarks on the stagnation thesis. How much is there in it? Is Keynes's Day of Judgment, or anything like it, at hand, in this country, in the United States, in the world at large? I do not think our monetary studies need cause us to modify greatly the views which we formed when discussing the 'real' theory of capital last term. Evidently we must not be too uplifted by the fact that since 1945, as a result of war and war finance, there has been a huge back-log both of consumption and of investment demand which has taken a long time to work off, and that that pressure has been reinforced by a heavy dose of rearmament. These pressures have from time to time begun to show signs of coming to an end; so let us remind ourselves of some of the reasons which have been advanced for long-run pessimism – the physical filling-up of the world, the declining rate of population growth, the unresponsiveness of some kinds of capital outlay to a falling interest rate. But let us remind ourselves also of three considerations on the other side.

(1) It is not at all clear that populations which are increasing in wealth per head *do* tend to consume a diminishing proportion of their income. It is dangerous to argue from the behaviour of the individual in this respect to that of the community whose composition is continually changing; each new generation seems to be pretty quick to adjust its spending habits to its improved opportunities. In America 'what the estimates seem to indicate is a constant long-run relation between income, investment and consumption since as far back as 1880.'[1] And as Schumpeter points out, a falling birth-rate, being associated psychologically with an increased propensity to enjoy life, cuts both ways in its effect on the demand for

[1] Williams, *Financing American Prosperity*, p. 365.

waiting and for labour. (But in point of fact the U.S. population is still increasing rapidly, – by some 2 per cent or 3 million persons a year.)

(2) Many kinds of capital outlay – docks, railways, office accommodation, nuclear reactors and the like – are not closely geared, like the output of machines, to the demand for consumption goods, but depend on broadly conceived estimates of the progress of whole regions. And fortunately it is just these types of outlay which *are* admittedly sensitive to movements of the rate of interest. Models of capital growth which ignore capital *deepening* are obviously lacking in comprehensiveness and realism.

(3) Nobody has ever yet succeeded in predicting just what is round the corner in the way of invention and technical change. Hitherto the scientist and the technician and the pioneering entrepreneur have always turned out to have something up their sleeve which nobody could have confidently expected. If you have time, look up the balanced discussion by Schumpeter (*Business Cycles*, Vol. II, pp. 1032–8), who thinks indeed that the private enterprise system is doomed, but for other reasons, namely because the psychological environment has become too hostile for its effective functioning. In his expressive metaphor, the balloon will be found to have 'shrivelled, not from causes inherent to its structure, but because the gas was being sucked out of it'. And read once more for yourselves the passage which I read you last term[1] in which Marshall, standing without knowing it on the edge of the Petrol Age, predicted the smooth fall of the rate of interest to 2 per cent (*Official Papers*, p. 49). The future course of what I described last term as the tussle between Invention and Fecundity on the one hand and Affluence and Thrift on the other is wrapped in mystery!

[1] See Vol. II, p. 87, n.

V

THE RATE OF INTEREST AGAIN

My critique of Keynesian interest theory was intended, you will remember, primarily as a preliminary to an examination of the stagnation thesis in its monetary aspects. But having performed that task, I propose to indulge in three little appendices about the rate of interest which may help to throw further light on some of the points I have tried to make.

I

The first will be a brief study of a subject which Keynes in his book almost wholly ignores – the relation between long rates and short. I have been speaking, as he does, as though there were only one rate; and I must continue to simplify to the extent of speaking as though there were only two – we can think of them as the yield on a perpetual bond and the rate for a three-months' bill – whereas in fact of course there is a whole spectrum of rates for securities of different maturities.

I conceive of the relation between long and short rates in a free enterprise economy after this fashion.

(1) There is a gap between the normal long and the normal short rate, the latter standing below the former on the average by an amount which can be regarded partly as a measure of the extra trouble and inconvenience to the borrower of continually renewing short loans, and partly of the greater freedom of manoeuvre, or ease of disentangling himself without loss, which the short loan confers on the lender. If we regard the long rate as the rate *par excellence*, then in the case of short loans, as Fisher put it long ago (listed work, p. 210), 'the readiness or convenience takes the place of some of the interest'.

Since the Treasury Bill superseded the trade bill as the predominant form of short-term investment in this country, this normal gap can, I think, be taken to be well established, though for earlier periods, in spite of a common opinion to the contrary, it is surprisingly difficult to detect – look at the Union Corporation's Trade Cycles Chart – and Lavington even goes so far as to deny its existence.

(2) The short rate is usually more volatile in both directions than the long; and when it flies downwards, the gap between the two is increased, when it flies upwards the gap is diminished, perhaps (as often in England in the nineteenth century) becoming negative, i.e. the short rate standing above the long. Amplifying an arithmetical example given by Pigou (*Industrial Fluctuations*, p. 276), the bare bones of this part of the theory can be set out as follows – all rates of interest being expressed as fractions and compound interest being neglected.

Let p = normal long rate. x = actual long rate.

Let q = normal short rate. y = actual short rate.

Let the short rate be expected to stay at y for n years, and then go back at one jump to q. What is x?

The price of a £1 bond bearing interest p has moved from its normal level 1 to $\frac{p}{x}$. If I spend $\frac{p}{x}$ on such a bond and hold it for n years I shall have $np + 1$. If I spend the same sum on a succession of bills I shall have $\frac{p}{x}(ny + 1)$; but I shall also have received a 'convenience yield' worth $\frac{p}{x}[n(p - q)]$, for this element of superior attractiveness in the short investment does not cease just because the yields are away from normal. Thus for the attractiveness of the two courses to be equal, we must have

$$np + 1 = \frac{p}{x} \, n[(y+p-q)+1]$$

or $$x = \frac{p}{np+1} \, [n(y+p-q)+1]$$

e.g. if $p=4\%$, $q=3\%$, $n=5$,
then if $y=1\%$, $x=3\frac{2}{3}\%$ (the gap is nearly 3 times the normal size)
but if $y=4\frac{1}{5}\%$, x also$=4\frac{1}{5}\%$ (the gap disappears).

Now let us put rather a severe strain on our imaginations. Let us suppose that the only sort of 'bill' is a bank balance, yielding o per cent, so that $y=0$: that what is volatile is not the (non-existent) rate on such a bill, but the bond rate itself, and that it is volatile only downwards, i.e. is always thought to be below its 'true' level: and finally that such a bill is not thought to have any intrinsic 'convenience-advantage' over a bond, so that the $(p-q)$ factor representing that advantage vanishes from our equation. Our equation then becomes simply $np+1=\frac{p}{x}$,

or $x=\frac{p}{np+1}$, which can be written also $p=\frac{x}{1-nx}$, or, if x is small, approximately $p=x(1+nx)$.

We have met this before! It is none other than the equation lying behind Keynes's exposition (*General Theory*, p. 202) of his 'speculative' theory. It is worth while, I think, evolving it from the pre-Keynesian theory by this circuitous route, because it brings out clearly how queer are the assumptions involved, and also how at best all that has been effected is to evaluate x in terms of p, no light being thrown on what defines the absolute level of p or therefore of x.

(3) In the past the short rate has not only, as just explained, varied within wider limits than the long, but has also been much more susceptible to influence by the Monetary Authority, since banks, even Central Banks,

were shy of creating money in appreciable quantities by way of long-term loan or investment. From this it was tempting to argue that, given the causeway between the two markets assumed in the preceding argument, the causal movement along it was entirely from the short to the long; and some writers, such as Hicks and Kaldor, have done so. This seems to me a mistake; once more, for the true doctrine for a free enterprise economy, even one with a well-developed Central Banking system, we must, I think, go back to Marshall. 'It is obvious,' he writes (listed work, p. 255), 'that the mean rate of discount must be much under the influence of the mean rate of interest for long loans; which is determined by the extent and richness of the field for capital investment on the one hand, and on the other by the amount of capital seeking investment.' For instance, if there is a pressure of new issues, the long rate tends to rise, and 'speculators' who can move between the two markets tend to sell bills, or to fail to renew them as they run off, thus transmitting the pressure from the long market to the short. Conversely, if the banks are buying securities hard from the public, thus tending to lower the long rate, those who are selling the securities for Keynes's 'speculative' reason, i.e. because they think the rate will rise later, will tend to re-invest in bills instead of leaving the money idle, and thus transmit the downward pressure to the short rate. Thus there is two-way traffic along the speculative causeway; and in a free enterprise economy the long rate remains, in my opinion, the senior member of the partnership, since it is not believed that in the long run the Monetary Authority will use its powers of acting on the short rate otherwise than in conformity with the underlying conditions of demand for and supply of investable funds.

II

My second appendix will consist of a brief and highly

stylised account of the typical behaviour of the rate of
interest in a period of cumulative disturbance such as I
analysed earlier with the aid of the Cambridge monetary
equation. This, I hope, will bring out one or two new
points, as well as consolidating some old ones. We will
be content with one rate of interest, calling all obligations
to repay loans by the name 'bonds', and thinking of such
of them as are marketable as having a price which varies
inversely with the rate of interest, so that we can speak
indifferently of the rate of interest rising or of the price of
bonds falling.

Consider first the relation of the rate with M. If the
banks – spontaneously or under pressure – are taking the
initiative in expanding M, they must do so by increasing
their willingness to lend, in a broad sense; i.e. their action,
and the consequent rise in P and/or R, tends to be
associated initially with a fall in the rate of interest. But as
P and/or R rises the demand for investable funds expands
and the rate rises again. How far will it rise? The orthodox
Keynesian doctrine, at any rate as expounded by Mrs
Robinson (*Introduction to the Theory of Employment*, pp.
76–8) appears to be that it will be 'driven back towards'
the level at which it originally stood, but can never go
beyond it. I have never been able to see the reason for this
limitation, which seems to me in flagrant conflict with
recorded history. The true doctrine, I think, was stated
by Marshall (listed work, p. 257) many decades ago:
'The increase of currency increases the willingness of
lenders to lend in the first instance, and lowers the rate of
discount. But it afterwards raises prices and therefore
tends to increase discount. This latter movement is cumulative.' Thus even if an expansory movement starts from
the M end, the rate of interest may be found at the end
of it much higher than at the beginning. And if it starts
not with an increase of M but with a decrease of K – with
an increase of confidence which leads people to desire to

F

devote an increased proportion of resources to real investment and so raises the demand for investable funds — there
is of course no need even for the preliminary dip in the
rate of interest, — the new money comes forward from the
banks in response to a higher rate of interest, not through
the instrumentality of a lower one. Conversely, if a con-
tractionist process starts with an increase of K, there will be
a decline in the demand for investable funds, and a fall in
the rate of interest will be associated with a fall in prices.

That is the common-sense explanation of the fact that
movements in prices are normally correlated with movements in the rate of interest in the same direction. But
that is not quite the whole truth, and by way of varying
the medicine we may carry the story a little further in
high-brow terms of the state of preference for different
kinds of assets. The first key to a rather complicated story
is that for some holders money and bonds are partial
substitutes, because bonds possess, though in a lower
degree, some of those qualities of 'safety' and 'saleability'
which we attributed *par excellence* to money. Hence a
decline in K is very likely accompanied by a decline in this
desire to hold resources in the form of bonds. This,
however, would not by itself explain why, when K declines,
the price of bonds should *fall* in terms of money, but only
why it should not, like other prices, *rise*. To explain why
it should actually fall, we must have recourse to the further
consideration that, while bonds are a *partial* substitute for
money, they are by no means a *complete* substitute. For
they are lacking in the 'convenience' qualities of money, —
you cannot use them, as they stand, as you can money, to
pay a debt of any size in any quarter — they are only a
substitute for 'inactive' and not for 'active' money. Hence
it is natural that when business is brisk, and both bonds
and money are falling in attractiveness relatively to goods,
bonds should also fall relatively to money, i.e. that the
rate of interest should rise.

But from this same fact – that money and bonds are by
no means complete substitutes – it also follows that in
certain conjunctures a *rise* in interest may be associated
with a *fall* in prices. For at times of severe crisis nothing
but money, with its super-liquidity, will serve, and both
bonds and goods are thrown on to the market in order to
secure it.

That, however, is not the end of the complications. For
if bonds are a partial substitute for money, they are also a
partial substitute for real capital assets – both fixed capital
and stocks of goods at all stages – since like such assets
they earn an income. Hence in a time of declining business
prospects, when K increases and P is falling, the desire to
hold bonds may increase even more than the desire to hold
money, since unlike most money they offer a prospect of
yielding an income: and we get what I have called the
normal association of a *fall* in the rate of interest with a
fall in prices. But conversely, from the same fact – that
bonds, as income-yielders, are a partial substitute for real
capital goods – it follows that in a time of quietly reviving
confidence after a slump a gradual fall in the K of many
different types of economic subjects may show itself partly
in an increased desire to hold bonds and partly in an
increased desire to hold goods, so that we get for a time a
gentle rise in the price of bonds, i.e. a gentle fall in the
rate of interest, associated with a gentle rise in prices –
the College Bursars plucking up heart to buy bonds and
the merchants to buy goods.

The whole matter may be set out in highly schematic
form as follows:

	S	L	S	L
	Early Recovery[1]	*Expansion*[2]	*Crisis*[3]	*Recession*[4]
Prices ...	Rise	Rise	Fall	Fall
Interest ...	Fall	Rise	Rise	Fall

[1] Both bonds and goods preferred to money.
[2] Goods preferred to money and money to bonds.
[3] Money preferred both to bonds and goods.
[4] Bonds preferred to money and money to goods.
S = short time-stretches.
L = long time-stretches.

I had better, however, add one caution about this model. It stylises away not only the difference between long and short rates, but also the difference between gilt-edged rates and industrial or risk-carrying rates of all shades, including, at the extreme end of the spectrum, that relation between current dividends and terms of issue which, in the case of new ordinary shares, takes the place of a rate of interest proper. The confidence of lenders varies no less than the confidence of borrowers. In time of slump, by no means everybody can get hold of invest-able funds by paying the gilt-edged rate; and in time of boom by no means everybody need pay the gilt-edged rate in order to get hold of investable funds. Hence my model, with its emphasis on the congruence between price-movements and interest-movements in the 'long' time-stretches 2 and 4, gives a somewhat unduly flattering picture of the stabilising influence of movements in 'the rate of interest' on industrial activity.

III

Now, as a third appendix to my treatment of the rate of interest, I want, without getting too deeply involved in topical problems, to offer some remarks on its behaviour in a controlled or directed economy, with special reference to the 'cheap money' policy which was pursued, with varying degrees of intensity, both in England and in the United States from the early 1930s until recently. So let us take up the story of the rate where we left it last term,[1] namely at the end of the 1920s, when it stood at about $4\frac{1}{2}$ per cent.

In the pre-war section of the ensuing period, except in one respect, the course of events conformed, I think, very closely to the neo-classical theory which I expounded last term. As I see it, in the early '30s the real forces were all on the side of a pronounced fall in the rate from its high

[1] See Vol. II of this series, p. 87.

post-first-war level; and the British authorities did little more than cash in, admittedly with great technical skill, on the operation of these real forces, the crucial step being the conversion in 1932 of the great block of 5 per cent War Loan to a 3½ per cent basis. And in so acting they were, as far as I can see, very little hampered by any pronounced elasticity of the 'speculative' pseudo-liquidity curve, the investing public, as Keynes himself says (*General Theory*, p. 204), pretty readily adjusting its expectations to the changed situation. But when, towards the end of the decade, the Authorities tried to go further, and to maintain the downward pressure in the face of rearmament and booming trade, the real forces turned round and hit them in the face; and it was not till war brought autocracy that the 3 per cent basis for Government borrowing was successfully established.

One feature in this period was, however, new – the prolonged and yawning gap, of more than 2½ per cent, between the long rate and the short, which I suppose was primarily due to the collapse of the international trade bill, leaving the Government without serious competitors as a borrower in the short market.

After the war, of course, everything was changed. The public were definitely put under notice that the Government intended to continue indefinitely to attempt to regulate not only the supply of money but also the demand for investable funds, relying for the purpose on a whole battery of financial and physical controls. Now that obviously makes a great difference; clearly you stand a much better chance of putting a price where you want it if you can not only influence the supply side of the market but also manage the demand side by shutting off competing demands. One can perhaps generalise the whole matter in this sort of way: the 'speculative motive' has no great importance if the Authorities are content, as they were in the early '30s, to operate in conformity with fundamental economic forces; it becomes important if it is felt that the Authorities are flying vainly in the face of those forces; but it seems not impossible that it should be reduced again to impotence if they can create the conviction that they are determined at all hazards to supersede the operation of those forces.

It was, I imagine, in this hope that, as you know, an attempt was made in this country not merely to hold, in the face of reconstruction demands, the 3 per cent rate established during the war, but to advance beyond it to the $2\frac{1}{2}$ per cent line, compelling the banks to create so much additional money – it turned out to be of the order of £900 millions – as might be necessary, in the light of the operation of the 'speculative' motive, to achieve this result, and trusting that in due course the market would become 'conditioned' – to use the fashionable modern phrase – to the new rate and that the 'speculative motive' would atrophy. My comment in these lectures on this policy when it was in its last phases (May 1947) seems to have been somewhat after this fashion (I won't swear this is a verbal quotation):

'I personally remain sceptical as to whether the game is worth the candle. A rate of interest thus shielded from the impact of private demand loses all function as an indicator of what is and what is not a sensible use of the community's limited power of enduring abstinence; and the threat to the standard of value involved in a cheap money policy *à outrance* is, I suspect, much greater than many enthusiastic advocates of that policy have allowed themselves to believe.'

I think the great body of responsible opinion has now come round to that view, though it is one which for some time seemed to be being left to the financial journalists rather than either the professional economists or the bankers, still less the then political Opposition, to uphold, – and though I believe that even in academic circles there are still *some* people who hold that all that was wrong with Dr Dalton was that he got cold feet. Anyway, cold feet were got; the ultra-cheap money policy came to grief, and, the retreat from 2½ per cent having begun, nobody was too clear when or where or why it should stop! Writing at the end of 1948 (*Utility and All That*, p. 95), I asked somewhat diffidently for 3½ per cent, though I think I knew in my bones that was still far too low. Anyway, having learnt to be thankful for small mercies, I was relieved when in the summer of 1949 the Labour Government allowed without serious resistance a slow upward drift to that level, though they went far to stultify their own action by declining to apply the new higher rate to their own loans to the Local Authorities.

In November 1951 the new Government faced such a further advance in the long rate, by then nearly 4 per cent, as was likely to be involved by their adoption of a more restrictive and flexible monetary policy, of which more in a moment, and even at last applied the higher rate to Local Authority borrowing, though for a time they continued to dribble the ball towards their own goal by monkeying about with the housing subsidies to match. In the little recession of 1953, under the combined influence of real and confidence forces, the rate slipped back to 3¾ per cent, but with the renewed boom and the credit squeeze of 1954–6 it has risen again to its 1929 level of over 4½ per cent. There let us leave it for the moment while we look across the Atlantic.

In the post-war boom in the United States, all the instruments of the Federal Reserve System for the control of inflation were seriously blunted by the fact that their use had to be subordinated to the overriding objective of what was described as 'maintaining an orderly market for Government securities'. As this phrase was interpreted in practice, it meant that not only the member banks but outside bodies such as insurance companies could at any time get hold of almost unlimited funds by unloading on to the Federal Reserve Banks, at rigidly pegged prices, Government securities of all maturities. The whole story, which is much complicated both by technicalities and by personal and jurisdictional issues between the authorities of the Treasury and the Federal Reserve System, was late in 1949 dragged into the light of day by a Congressional Sub-Committee under the chairmanship of the well-known economist Senator Paul Douglas, whose report, accompanied by the usual American spate of memoranda and oral hearings, is very interesting reading. With the recession of 1948–9 the problem seemed temporarily to have lost urgency; but looking to the future, the Sub-Committee definitely recommended as follows:

'The advantages of avoiding inflation are so great that they should be pursued even if the cost is a significant increase in the service charges on the Federal debt and a greater inconvenience to the Treasury in its sale of securities for new financing and refunding purposes. In general, the Government ought not to use its monetary policy to maintain easy credit and to facilitate the management of its own debt if that monetary policy is not conducive to the maintenance of general economic stability. . . . Flexibility of interest rates, without which a flexible monetary policy is impossible, should be restored.'

With the trade recovery of 1949, followed by the Korean boom, the problem became urgent again, and as a result of a much-publicised Accord between the Treasury and the Federal Reserve Board in March 1951, the latter's automatic support of the bond market was withdrawn. Shortly afterwards a new sub-committee, of which Douglas was a member but Representative Patman, who held diametrically opposite views, chairman, considered the whole matter afresh, took 1,300 pages of fresh evidence, and – Mr Patman apparently behaving with great moderation – broadly confirmed the earlier body's conclusions. (I tell my American friends that the dirty linen which in America is washed in public by Congressional committees is in England handled at a secret laundry in Ludgate Circus – half-way between Whitehall and Threadneedle Street.)

Under the new régime, the Federal Reserve continues to admit some responsibility for what it now describes as 'correcting disorderly conditions' in the Government bond market, but insists that such considerations must not be allowed to interfere with its main function of promoting stability in the level of activity through controlling credit. There is in the United States no *fully* long-term rate corresponding to the yield on irredeemable Consols or Daltons, but the yield on the longest security outstanding – 3 per cent 1995 bonds issued in February 1955 – was in the spring of 1957 over $3\frac{1}{4}$ per cent.

Finally, as an appendix to this appendix, let me add a word on the relation, in a controlled or semi-controlled economy, between the long rate and the short. A completely successful policy of stabilising the long rate at a low level would presumably lead ultimately to the virtual disappearance of the gap between the two rates; for if it is certain that bonds will always be able to be unloaded without trouble at a fixed price, not only any abnormal spread due to both rates being below the believed normal, but also the normal spread due to the superior disentangleability of lending short, would have become anachronisms. Clearly during the cheap-money régime in this country this never happened; for as you know the short rate was not allowed to rise appreciably above the $\frac{1}{2}$ per cent level at which it was pegged at the end of the war; so that the yawning and persistent gap which, as I have said, first appeared in the 1930s, had by November 1951 widened to nearly $3\frac{1}{2}$ per cent. In this respect the policy of the British Authorities had differed from that of their opposite numbers in the United States, who permitted their short rates to rise somewhat even when they were continuing to resist a rise in the long rate.

With some £5,000 millions of floating debt outstanding the fiscal motive for continuing to sit firmly on the head of the short rate is obviously very strong. At the same time I have always found it hard to see how any serious policy of restoring vitality to the interest rate could stop short of abandoning the attempt to block permanently those natural causeways which, I have argued, run from the long rate to the short. And it has seemed to me that if they persisted in this attempt the Authorities would find that they were rendering the long rate *more* vulnerable to movements of confidence than it need be, by denying elasticity to those short rates which used to serve it as a sort of mobile screen or lightning conductor.

I therefore thoroughly approved of the steps taken by the Authorities in November 1951 to stiffen up the terms of short-term lending; but, while I think it was natural that they should start with a moderate action, designed to establish the principle of flexibility rather than to administer a spectacular shock, I found myself becoming increasingly critical during the next three years of the apparent lack of seriousness with which the new monetary policy was being pressed. Of the deeper reasons for this, especially the implications of the doctrine of 'full employment', I shall have more to say later; for the moment I want to stick to the more technical matter of the relation between the various rates of interest. It seemed to me that the Authorities were trusting too much to the general semaphore effects of a raised Bank rate, and to the direct effect of the associated rise in the rates for bank advances in deterring borrowers, and were evading the function of the role of the interest rate in determining the basis of credit. For while they had reasserted the rights of the Old Lady to charge a penal rate to the bill-brokers for discounting their bills, she was not in fact, except very occasionally, doing so, but was continuing to exude money on a sufficiently generous scale to put no obstacle in the way of Government borrowing by Treasury Bill at a rate which never rose as high as 2½ per cent and in the summer of 1954 was no more than 1¾ per cent. It was not till the semi-crisis of sterling in early 1955 that the Bank rate was not only yanked up to 4½ per cent but at last made really effective, the bill-brokers being 'put into the Bank' in the good old style and kept there, and the Government reconciling itself at last to paying 4 per cent on its Treasury Bills, – a figure which rose at times during 1956 to over 5 per cent – ten times the pre-1951 level.

And even now the position is far from stable. What has in fact become increasingly plain is that the success with which in the old days the Bank of England contrived to combine the roles of controller of the money supply and unconditional lender of last resort to the market depended on the fact that the type of borrower with whom she was most closely – though even so, indirectly – in touch was the drawer of commercial bills of exchange, who was highly sensitive to the pressure of interest rates. A Treasury which is *not* thus sensitive – which is determined to go on meeting its long-term capital expenditure by drawing bills, whatever the rate – can always aid and abet the commercial banks in kicking back at a Central Bank which is trying to constrict their credit base. Having reached the conclusion that if you want to check inflation it is no use letting the long rate go up unless you let the short rates go up as well, we are now driven on to a further conclusion, namely that it is no use letting the short rates go up unless you are prepared to let the long rate go up further to the extent that is necessary in order to permit the Government to fund a considerable proportion of its short-term debt and so relax the pressure of its demands on the short-term market. *If* that can be successfully achieved, then we may expect to see the normal pattern of rates restored, with the Consols rate well above the bill rate instead of nearly equal to or – as in 1956 – actually below it. Let me refer again to the important – and by no means easy – articles on this subject by King, Dacey and Sayers which I have listed. I may add that I am by no means myself convinced that the pursuit of this objective necessarily demands the actual lowering of Bank rate and the short-term rates associated with it while inflation is still rife, however much such lowering may be accompanied by assurances that it is not intended as a green light.

Anyway we seem to reach the conclusion that under present conditions an Authority which sets out to control the supply of money through a banking system must concern itself with the level of the long-term rate of interest as well as the short. But it is worth noting that this question has lately been the subject of acute controversy in the United States, not this time between the Treasury and the Federal Reserve System but between the constituent parts of the latter. The Board in Washington has taken the view that the System can achieve its objects by confining its dealings to the short market, and that intervention in the long market runs the risk of undoing the good done by the 1951 Accord, of rendering the System subservient to the Treasury, and of interfering with the development of a free and active bond market. The New York Bank, which has to do the actual work, has taken the view that it cannot rely on the automatic transmission of its pressures from the short market to the long, and must be allowed to deal directly with the latter as well; this, it argues, involves no greater degree of 'interventionism' than Congress has sanctioned by setting up the System in the first instance. In a sprightly article in the *Three Banks Review* (March 1956), Samuelson comes down on the side of the Bank, and I must say I agree with him.

VI

THE TRADE CYCLE: WHAT HAPPENS

After this long excursus, let me take you back to the main
theme of our discourse – the meaning of monetary equilibrium, the policies necessary to preserve it in a progressive economy, and the obstacles with which such policies
are confronted. Whatever view we take about the long-run
outlook, there seems no reason to doubt that many of the
points which we discussed in connection with the
'stagnation thesis' are relevant to conditions of pronounced
industrial depression; and our task in these final lectures
is to re-examine our principles of monetary policy with
reference not to a stably progressing economy, but to one
which has already become a prey to fluctuation.

I propose to begin by describing, in a rather common-
sense and low-brow way, the course of a typical industrial
fluctuation, so far as history can be said to reveal the
existence of such a thing. I shall use the present tense,
without thereby meaning to prejudice the question
whether, whatever other horrors the future may hold in
store, these particular troubles can now be regarded as
'part and parcel of the dreadful past'.

Starting from a more or less mean position of activity –
for we must start somewhere – a further upward thrust
may occur for any one of a number of reasons. It may
occur to meet a demand arising out of abundant harvests,
either directly, through the farmers' purchases of equipment and the like, or indirectly, via the pressure on railway
and shipping capacity, or more indirectly still, through the
optimism generated as to the prospects of the producing
areas. Or it may be provoked by the discovery of a 'new'
country; or by the desire to exploit a new invention, or a

new application of an old one. Historically, it seems possible to connect most of the 'nineteenth century' (i.e. 1815–1914) booms with one or more of these events – metallurgy, steam, electricity, petrol, successively playing leading parts; the countries of South America proving capable of being discovered over and over again as though Cortez and Pizarro had never existed; and the fluctuations in Nature's bounty playing a role which is none the less recognisable because it may not be possible to reduce it to a regular cyclical pattern closely linked with the peculiar maladies which afflict our glorious Sun. Much the same can be said of the boom of 1925–9, the 'new' countries on this occasion being largely the 'renewable' countries of war-shattered Europe; while the boom of 1919–20, and again that of 1936–7 in the United States, seem to have been largely a matter of rapid re-stocking with *working* capital.

But it is not impossible that recovery beyond the norm should be simply the extension of a preceding recovery process, involving the re-absorption of unemployed factors of production and the expansion of consuming power. It does not make much difference whether the expansion originates in the instrumental trades and is communicated to the consumption trades through increased purchasing power, according to what when I was young was called the 'principle of repercussion' and is now called the principle of the multiplier; or whether it starts in the consumption trades and is communicated to the instrumental trades through the derived demand for new equipment, according to the principle which when I was young was thought too obvious to require a name, but which later came to be called the 'principle of acceleration', and which Harrod, when he discovered it all over again for himself, christened with the rather ambiguous term 'the relation'. In either case idle money is sucked into use; and the aid of the banks is sought for building up an

abnormally large proportion of an abnormally large increment of working capital, and also, so far as they can
be induced to desert their avowed principles – which to
some extent they can – for building up fixed capital as
well.

Thus a process of rising prices and 'forced levies' is set
in motion, a process which, owing to the length of time
which it takes to bring new instruments to birth, is as a
rule only partly mitigated by the expansion of consumable
output, and which is apt to be exaggerated by several
factors, some of which I will proceed to enumerate.

(i) The period of process for which goods require
financing is lengthened, owing both to physical con-
gestions and delays at all stages, and sometimes to the
holding back of goods from market by speculators in
the hope of a further rise in prices.

(ii) The emergence of windfall profits generates optimism in entrepreneurs and furnishes an additional
stimulus, beyond the original stimulus, to expansion of
output. To some extent this optimism is irrational –
people are slow to realise that other people's selling-prices
will rise as well as their own; but to some extent it is
perfectly rational, since the prices at which they can hire
the other factors of production, including the use of
investable funds, are relatively sticky.

(iii) In the face of rising prices, the fixed income folk
may draw down their money balances in the attempt to
maintain their standards of consumption, thus decreasing K.

(iv) There is a tendency for entrepreneurs to borrow
in order to finance, not merely extensions of production
but the consumption of increments of personal capital
wealth. Thus take a merchant who with a bank loan of
£1,000 has bought and handled goods for £1,000 and
sells them on a rising market for £1,100. It is not im-
probable that he will try to cash in on this paper gain by

spending the £100 and persuading the bank to scale up
his loan on the plea that prices have risen. Thus the banks
will be under pressure to create new money not merely
to finance extensions of working capital but to prevent
existing stocks of working capital from being depleted.
The probability of this is increased by the fact that in
many cases the stock of working capital does not remain
continuously in one hand – the farmer sells wheat to
repay his loan while the miller borrows to take the wheat
over. Thus we may have the farmer repaying his £1,000
and quietly blowing the windfall £100, while the miller
legitimately argues that he must have £1,100 from the
bank in order to buy the wheat. The importance of this
source of inflammation is increased under modern tax
conditions and at modern tax levels, since the windfall-
receiving entrepreneur, however thrifty his own habits,
will have to hand over a handsome proportion of his
windfall as tax for the State to spend.

In every inflammatory process of this kind the expansion of its loans appears to the bank as a *result* not a *cause*
of the rise in prices. No banker takes easily to the proposition which I advanced some lectures ago – that if his
action is an *essential condition* for a certain state of affairs
continuing to happen, it is legitimate, if one is concerned
with remedial measures, to treat it as the *cause*.

(v) The same kind of thing as I have just described
as happening in the commodity markets happens also in
the capital market, new money being in effect created to
finance capital gains which are used by the recipient to
expand his consumption.

How is this cumulative upward process stopped and
reversed? It seems to me unlikely that there is a single
answer applicable to all occasions; there is a great variety
of reasons why, in Haberler's language, the system may
become more and more sensitive to 'deflationary shocks'
as expansion proceeds. Some interpreters have laid stress

on purely monetary factors – the fact that the banks, finding their reserves slipping away through withdrawals of legal tender money to pay the enhanced wage-bills, etc., ultimately draw in their horns with a jerk. Others lay stress on the emergence of what they call a 'shortage of saving', which no liberality on the part of the banks could remedy. According to this picture, windfall profits are eaten into by rising wages and interest rates, which at this stage no longer lag appreciably behind the rise in prices, and with the disappearance of windfall profits the main source of demand for instrumental goods is dried up. There turns out to be an overproduction of such goods in the sense, as Cassel puts it, of 'an overestimate of the . . . amount of savings available for taking over the real capital produced'. Others again, however, declare that more saving could no more avert the turning-point than could more bank credit, since the real trouble is the temporary exhaustion of investment opportunities. If consumption has made the pace, then a mere decline in the rate of increase of consumption, such as must occur when most unemployed persons have been re-absorbed into employment, will produce an absolute decline in the demand for new machines. If construction has made the pace, then once the new railway system or mercantile marine has been built, once the new South American republic has been fitted out, there occurs a condition of saturation which will not be worked off for several years. For not only does a once-for-all installation suffice to meet the repetition, year by year, of the new raised rate of demand, but – worse than that – many kinds of fixed capital are of such a lumpy and discontinuous character that, if they are installed at all, they must be installed on a scale which will suffice to cater not only for existing demand but for the probable *increment* of demand over a number of years.

One's outlook on the causes of relapse is apt, I think, to be coloured by the nature of the first relapse which one

G

remembers hearing or reading about. In my case that is the spectacular crash of 1907, which, like its predecessor of 1873 (which I may say I *don't* remember), lends itself fairly easily to description in terms of a 'shortage of saving' or, what comes to much the same thing, of an output of instrumental goods which is disproportionately large relatively to that of consumption goods having regard to the volume of saving – perhaps I had better guard myself like a White Paper by saying 'genuine' saving – available. Even so my own view, on record in my book written in 1912–14, has always been that even when shortage of credit or 'shortage of saving' is the actual operative cause of relapse, the third cause which I have distinguished, namely temporary saturation with important groups of capital instruments, is frequently the most important underlying feature of the situation, and *would have* become operative before long even if the others hadn't. And most modern discussion of the turning-point is naturally coloured by memories of that of 1929, which ushered in the great super-slump of 1929–32, and which in many ways was markedly different from its predecessors of 1872 and 1907 and 1920. The long previous expansion in the United States, from 1922 – with minor setbacks – to 1929, had many peculiar features, especially the failure of *prices* to rise significantly; and certainly one way of interpreting it is to suppose that cyclical expansion was superimposed on certain non-cyclical depressive features, especially the rapid technological improvements in agriculture, tending to produce saturation of particular demands, and the 'deflationary' changes in my fractions b and D to which I drew attention in discussing the theory of banking. Perhaps, too, the real cyclical expansion was over by 1927 – many kinds of construction had already reached saturation point – and it might have been the lesser evil to acquiesce in a moderate recession at that date than to attempt, as was in fact done, to re-galvanise the

expansion by a cheap money policy which proved in-
effective as a treatment of the non-cyclical features of the
situation and served only to generate a wild stock exchange
boom, which led in turn to a quite unnecessarily violent
collapse of the whole financial and economic structure.

But I must not pursue that particular story further,[1]
but return to my generalised treatment.

Once the recession has started, for whatever reason,
it will tend to be intensified by cumulative influences
which are the counterpart of those which develop during
a boom. The relative stickiness of wages and interest rates
generates windfall losses instead of windfall profits;
pessimism, rational and irrational, takes the place of
optimism, rational and irrational. The fixed income folk,
becoming relatively well off, are likely to take the opportunity to reconstitute their balances, thus further increasing the average K for the whole community; though
an effect in the other direction will be exercised by consumption in excess of income both by unemployed persons
and by entrepreneurs depleting their balances for the
purpose or selling securities, and thus diverting into the
finance of consumption some thrift on the part of others
which would otherwise in the circumstances have gone
completely to waste.

As regards the banks, the parallel between boom and
slump is not complete. We saw that on a rising market
the miller will want to borrow more than the farmer is
repaying. On a falling market the miller, it is true, will
want to borrow less than the farmer borrowed; but the
farmer may well want to borrow the amount of his capital
loss. Thus unless the banks are ruthless, or themselves
collapse, as they did in the United States on a grand scale
in 1930-2, what are described as 'frozen credits' will
remain outstanding, and the volume of bank money may

[1] For two suggestive versions of it, see J. M. Clark, *Strategic Factors in Business
Cycles*, pp. 96-123, and T. Wilson, *Fluctuations in Income and Employment*, Part II.

sink but slowly. This phenomenon, like other forms of borrowing, will check the fall in money income; but it will be in danger of preserving plague-spots in the economic system and impairing the power of the banks to initiate recovery by making new loans in directions which are *not* saturated. Very difficult and delicate is the task of the banker in deciding who should be nursed through a bad period and who squeezed out.

About the lower turning-point it is as hard to generalise as about the upper. In the absence of other recuperative forces the need to replace both instruments of production and the more durable kinds of consumption goods, if economic life is to continue, tend to set a bottom to the depression; though we must remember our discovery in the October term that 'the short period is not the same length at both ends', the length of life of many instruments being many times as great as their period of gestation. More often recovery seems to start with a gradual re-growth of confidence among the consumption trades, the construction trades coming along later in the manner described by Marshall (*Principles*, pp. 710–11), in that notable account of a trade depression which has been so neglected by some subsequent writers that I hope you'll forgive my reading it in full. Notice the rather odd way in which in the last two sentences the indicative mood replaces the conditional; what *would* happen quicker if there were more confidence, *does* nevertheless happen in the end.

'But though men have the power to purchase they do not always use it. For when confidence has been shaken by failures, capital cannot be got to start new companies or extend old ones. Projects for new railways meet with no favour, ships lie idle, and there are no orders for new ships. There is scarcely any demand for the work of navvies, and not much for the work of the building and engine-making trades. In short there is but little occupation in any of the trades which make fixed capital. Those whose skill and capital is specialized in these trades are earning little, and therefore buying little of the produce of other trades.

Other trades, finding a poor market for their goods, produce less; they earn less, and therefore they buy less: the diminution of the demand for their wares makes them demand less of other trades. Thus commercial disorganization spreads: the disorganization of one trade throws others out of gear, and they react on it and increase its disorganization.

'The chief cause of the evil is a want of confidence. The greater part of it could be removed almost in an instant if confidence could return, touch all industries with her magic wand, and make them continue their production and their demand for the wares of others. If all trades which make goods for direct consumption agreed to work on, and to buy each other's goods as in ordinary times, they would supply one another with the means of earning a moderate rate of profits and of wages. The trades which make fixed capital might have to wait a little longer: but they too would get employment when confidence had revived so far that those who had capital to invest had made up their minds how to invest it. Confidence by growing would cause itself to grow; credit would give increased means of purchase, and thus prices would recover. Those in trade already would make good profits, new companies would be started, old businesses would be extended; and soon there would be a good demand even for the work of those who make fixed capital. There is of course no form of agreement between the different trades to begin again to work full time, and so to make a market for each other's wares. But the revival of industry comes about through the gradual and often simultaneous growth of confidence among many various trades; it begins as soon as traders think that prices will not continue to fall: and with a revival of industry prices rise.'

Sometimes, however, there appears to be some more definite starting-point or rallying-point of recovery. It may be that some 'investment opportunity' which has only been temporarily saturated again raises a thirsty head – as for instance electricity, having been applied on a large scale in the 1890s to transport and lighting, took a new lease of life in the 1900s with its application to general manufacture. Or it may be a brand-new technical or organisational star – the petrol engine, the Suez Canal, the device of Limited Liability – which lights up the economic horizon and brings activity rapidly up to and past that mean or normal level – perhaps little more than a fleeting abstraction – at which we started to watch its behaviour.

VII

THE TRADE CYCLE: MODELS AND TOOLS

I don't myself feel sure that much has yet been added to such a low-brow account of the trade cycle as I have just given by the various mathematical models which have become fashionable in recent years. For a middle-brow scheme, using simple diagrams, I may refer you to No. 5 of my *Essays in Monetary Theory*; among high-brow ones I may mention Kalecki (No. 6 of *Essays in the Theory of Economic Fluctuations*); Kaldor (*E.J.*, March 1940); Samuelson (No. 12 of *Readings in Business Cycle Theory*); and what should now perhaps be regarded as the fine flower of the 'model' garden, Hicks's book *The Trade Cycle*. In addition notable attempts have been made by Tinbergen and other econometricians to weave actual data into a closed mathematical system.

My present feeling is that all these models do point the way to possible advances of theory beyond the comparative study of positions of short-period equilibrium outlined by Keynes and formalised by Pigou in his *Employment and Equilibrium*. At the same time I think they carry great dangers unless kept in control by a strong historical sense. For, given a few functions and a few lags, for anybody with the requisite mathematical skill (which I needn't, at this time of day, tell you that I lack) the construction of self-generating cycles is so easy that it is apt to inflict a tendency to overestimate the extent to which actual cycles *are* self-generating, and hence to under-estimate the part played by 'innovations' of all kinds and by the lumpiness and discontinuity of the processes of investment undertaken in response thereto.

To that general judgment I should like to add some

remarks on two of the principal tools which figure in these various kit-bags. The first is the so-called multiplier principle. As I understand it, the pure theory of the multiplier, when laid out properly in time, can be put in this wise. Let us – and it is important to make this plain at the outset – ignore for the purpose in hand the difference between real and money income, i.e. let us assume that output can be expanded within the relevant limits without change of price. Let there take place an addition N to the rate of capital outlay per small unit of time. Let there be in force a function relating the amount which people desire to consume in any small unit of time to their income received in the previous unit of time, this function being such that people spend a proportion q of any addition which has been made to their income in the previous unit of time. Then, in the first time interval in which the addition to capital outlay occurs, the addition to pre-existing total income will be N, in the next $N(1 + q)$, in the next $N(1 + q + q^2)$ and so forth, until it becomes, or becomes indistinguishable from, $N\dfrac{1}{1 - q}$, that being the sum of an infinite convergent series of this kind. While income is rising to this level, the ratio of additional income to additional capital outlay, as recorded by statistics, will be continually altering, and will always be *less* than $\dfrac{1}{1 - q}$; and if we use the word 'multiplier' we ought, I think, to make it plain to which of these two ratios the term is being applied – the ratio enshrining the psychological propensity, or the recorded quotient, additional income divided by additional capital outlay, in the actual time-interval under observation. We can describe the relation prevailing between saving and capital outlay during this period when income is increasing in such language as we think fit; but whatever terminology we use, it is essential to the model that the given income-consumption function is conceived of as being applied, in each time-unit, not to the income which is going to be received in that time-unit but to that which has been received in the previous time-unit. When income has reached $N\dfrac{1}{1-q}$, but not before, we have a self-renewing situation which can be reasonably described as one of equilibrium, or quasi-equilibrium, in the market for thrift.

Now this seems to me, when thus expressed, to be quite a self-consistent little piece of apparatus, worth setting out, so to speak, under a glass case in order to get clear about its implications. But let us consider some of the complications to be taken into account before trying to apply it to real life. In the first place, of course, while the model is working itself out all sorts of other things may be happening which will upset its operation: but that is a difficulty which besets all economic reasoning. But secondly, the very processes depicted are almost certain to set in motion forces modifying their own operation. Let me distinguish three separate instances of this.

(i) The increase in consumption is likely, under many conditions, to stimulate a further increase in capital outlay, – as I put it, in my early comment on the model (*Essays*, No. 9), 'dogs wag tails, as well as tails dogs'. For this reason alone it would not seem to be at all likely that, as a result of an original increase N in the rate of capital outlay, we should get a nice smooth convergent irreversible movement to an increased rate of income $\dfrac{N}{1-q}$. It would be all too probable that for a time the movement would be divergent and explosive, and that even if in the end a position of quasi-equilibrium were reached, with designed saving equal to planned capital outlay or however you like to put it, that position would be an evanescent one – a peak rather than a plateau. This of course is now recognised by those trade cycle theorists who seek to combine the multiplier principle with the principle of acceleration, to which we shall come later, in order to explain the actual course of events.

(ii) The function linking consumption with received income, presuming it to exist originally, may be changed by the working of the model. It may, for instance, be changed downwards, as a result of the enhanced proportion of income accruing to the rich entrepreneur class; or upwards, as a result of the propensity of members of that class to spend their increments of capital wealth, or of the re-encroachment of wages on profits as expansion proceeds.

(iii) The increase in saving may itself generate an increase in capital outlay. Modern thought rightly emphasises that the acts of saving and of capital outlay are often performed by different persons; but it is also true that they are frequently performed by the same 'person', namely a business; and the amount of capital outlay actually done by firms is likely, in my view, in the real world to depend a good deal on how much they are able to save. Thus not all the additional saving done in each time-unit will be available to finance the original programme N of additional capital outlay per time-unit – some of it will walk off on its own to finance some quite different kind of additional capital outlay.

I have been much interested to see that high-brow opinion has at last become alive to this possibility – high-brow opinion, you know, is like a hunted hare; if you stand long enough in the same place, or nearly the same place, it is apt to come round to you in a circle. Mr Kalecki, than whose no brow is higher, has revealed in an article in the *Review of Economic Studies*, No. 40 (1949–50), with the high-sounding title of 'A New Approach to the Problem of Business Cycles', that he has become dissatisfied with the explanations currently given of the behaviour of capital outlay in the trade cycle in terms of the principle of acceleration and so forth. As a substitute he offers the following thought: 'A reasonable interpretation of the inter-relation between the level of income and investment decisions should be based, I think, on the fact that with the high level of income there is correlated a high level of savings, and that the stream of new savings stimulates investment because it makes it possible to undertake investment without increasing indebtedness.' The wheel has come full circle. If you want to be really up to date you can now say that it is not so much investment which governs savings as savings which govern investment. But you had better be careful to give Mr Kalecki as your authority, otherwise you may be suspected of vulgar schoolboy error.

Finally, consider what happens to the multiplier principle when, as is presumably normally the case, the supply of consumption goods is not perfectly elastic. In this case the real multiplier is less, the money multiplier greater, than $\dfrac{1}{1-q}$. Let us concentrate on the extreme case when the supply of consumption goods is completely inelastic. The real multiplier is now obviously 1 — real output increases by the increase, if any, in the output of investment goods and no more. In evaluating the money multiplier it becomes relevant that the consumption function is commonly assumed (i) to be given in real terms, (ii) to be of the form $c = a + qy$, a being a fixed element independent of real income, so that a man with no income will nevertheless exercise some consumption by living on savings or getting into debt. Let our original price level of consumption goods be 1, so that y can stand for original money income and also for its value in terms of consumption goods. Then, N being the additional money capital outlay per unit of time as before, in period 1 total money income only rises by N and in period 2 by qN, prices not having yet risen. But during period 2 the price level of consumption goods rises to $1 + \dfrac{qN}{a+qy}$, and therefore in period 3 enough money[1] will be spent on consumption goods to raise total money income by $qN\left(\dfrac{a}{a+qy}+q\right)$ instead of by q^2N. The whole series of money income increases, while it will still be convergent, will have a sum $N\dfrac{1}{1-\dfrac{a}{y}-q}$, which is greater than $N\dfrac{1}{1-q}^2$.

All this, however, is on the assumption that the additional capital outlay – additional, that is, over what was going on before the story started – remains unchanged in each period at N, in spite of the rise in the price of consumption goods. What this means, of course, is either that those making the capital goods must be content to work for a smaller and smaller real reward, or that, for the given rate of capital outlay, a smaller and smaller volume of physical investment is performed. If neither of these conditions is fulfilled, i.e. if the capital outlay is to be taken as given in terms of volume and not of money, and if those who produce it insist on seeing their money incomes go up *pari passu* with those of the rest of the community, then the series explodes.

These complications are frequently hidden from view in *simpliste* exposition of the theory of the multiplier, which, like so much of the rest of the analysis of which it forms part, becomes a somewhat treacherous guide to policy once we leave conditions of extreme depression.

As is well known, the first attempts which were made to

---

[1] This follows from the assumptions of the story; I leave the reader to worry it out by simple algebra.

[2] I am grateful to Prof. Hicks for guiding my faltering steps to this conclusion. Happily Prof. Goodwin, though making a different assumption about lags, had already reached the same result! *The New Economics*, p. 497.

use the concept of the consumption function for purposes of prediction and policy were not happy — everybody has heard of the phantom army of 8 million unemployed which it succeeded in churning out in the United States in the spring of 1946. Since then a great deal of high-grade and devoted ability has been lavished on the attempt to make it more ship-shape and serviceable; and I do not wish to speak disrespectfully of these efforts. Attempts are now made by some writers to take account of the probability that people's spending plans in any short period of time depend not only on their income but on their capital resources, and especially on their capital resources in money or other fairly liquid forms. Others suggest that the relation between a man's spending plans and his immediately past, or as for this purpose we may without danger say his current, income will be different according as to whether that current income is the highest he has ever known or has sunk from some previous higher level. Thus if we write S for current saving, Y for current income and Y_0 for the highest income previously known, Mr Duesenberry[1] claims to have discovered by econometric methods that the current form of the consumption function in the United States is (if I may rough his arithmetic) $\dfrac{S}{Y} = \dfrac{1}{4} \cdot \dfrac{Y}{Y_0} - \dfrac{1}{5}$. This gives the attractive result that if income is gently increasing in a normal year, so that $\dfrac{Y}{Y_0} = \dfrac{104}{100}$, the proportion of income saved is about 6 per cent, but may become markedly less in a slump, when people are trying to maintain something like the level of consumption reached in the previous boom. For instance, if income sinks as much as one-fifth below its boom level, so that $\dfrac{Y}{Y_0} = \dfrac{4}{5}$, saving becomes zero.

[1] *Income, Saving and the Theory of Consumer Behaviour.*

Duesenberry also makes the alternative suggestion that what a man saves depends not so much on how his income behaves absolutely as on how it behaves relatively to those of other people, so that if his income increases he will not save a larger proportion of it if other people's incomes have increased in the same proportion, so that he still finds himself in the same position in the income-scale, with the same number of people above him whose expenditure and habits he wishes to emulate.

Both these hypotheses, as well as simpler ones, can be offered as explanations of the observed fact, to which I have already drawn attention, that the proportion of income saved by a whole community does not seem necessarily to increase over decades as the community grows richer – a fact which, as I have already suggested, seems to remove one of the linch-pins from the stagnation thesis. But unless and until these various modifications of the simpliste multiplier concept can be effectively sorted and tested out, that concept must remain, it seems to me, an extremely unreliable instrument for short-run or cyclical prediction.

I can deal more briefly with the companion piece of furniture – the acceleration principle. In my general account of the trade cycle, I laid great stress on the *lumpiness* of investment – on the fact that a rise in the rate of final demand may stimulate the installation of an instrument which will be capable not only of looking after the raised rate of demand in future years as well as in the present year, but also, sometimes, of looking after a *further* rise in the rate of demand. And I have always felt that it is to the acceleration principle, interpreted in this broad way, that one should give pride of place in one's thoughts about the cycle. But it seems to me that there are at least as many traps here as in the case of the multiplier in the way of reducing the concept to a smooth, continuous, functional basis.

Let me start by illustrating the principle in its crudest form.

Year	Con- sumption	Needed Plant	Replace- ment	Additional Plant	Total output of capital goods
1	100	400	20	—	20
2	110	440	20	40	60
3	115	460	20?+	20	40?+

We start with a stable position in which annual expenditure on consumption goods is £100, of which £20 is devoted to replacing $\frac{1}{20}$ of a fixed capital plant worth £400; i.e. the ratio of fixed capital to annual output of consumption goods is 4. All fixed capital is supposed to be employed up to capacity. In year 2 the demand for consumption goods rises by £10; in order to satisfy it, £40 of additional plant must be installed, i.e. total demand for new capital goods rises from £20 to £60 – an increase of 10 per cent in demand for consumption goods has led to an increase of 200 per cent in the demand for new capital goods. In year 3 demand for consumption goods rises by another £5, i.e. by only about $4\frac{1}{2}$ per cent: to satisfy it £20 of additional plant must be installed, i.e. total demand for new capital goods *falls* from £60 to £40, or perhaps just a little over £40 if some of the new plant installed in year 2 already requires replacement. Thus the actual demand for capital goods depends on the *rate of increase* of demand for consumption goods; and it is easy to see how, given a cyclical upward swing in the demand for consumption goods, this principle could operate so as, first, to cause the amplitude of the swing to be greater for capital than for consumption goods and, secondly, to cause the turning-point to come earlier for capital than for consumption goods, the effect appearing to precede the cause. Further, the principle applies to some extent to working capital as well. Thus suppose a merchant is selling 100 units of goods a week, ordering 100 in replacement from the manufacturer, and keeping 2,000, i.e.

20 weeks' sales, in stock. Suppose now the rate of weekly demand rises from 100 to 110 and is expected to remain at that level. He will need to bring his stocks as quickly as possible up to 2,200. Suppose he does it all in the second week, his orders from manufacturers will rise in that week from 100 to 310, but will thereafter sink again to 110. Thus the principle can be invoked to show why demand should fluctuate more for primary products than for manufactured output and more for manufactured output than for goods at retail, and to throw light on those shorter 'inventory' cycles of which, especially in the United States, several sometimes seem to be contained within the ambit of a single longer cycle moulded by the behaviour of fixed capital.

But of course in looking for evidence of the working of the principle in real life we must remember several things. First, fixed capital is not always, or perhaps often, fully employed, so that the impact of increased demand will be felt partly – and to a different extent at different stages of the cycle – in securing fuller employment rather than in impelling the creation of new plant. Secondly, the principle does not operate symmetrically downwards. To see this we need another table.

Year	Con- sumption	Needed Plant	Replace- ment	Actual Plant at end year	Total output of capital goods
1	100	400	20	400	20
2	90	360	—	380	—
3	80	320	—	360	—
	85	340	—	360	—

Let us suppose the drop of 10 per cent in consumption in year 2 causes all replacement to be suspended, i.e. reduces output of capital goods by 100 per cent. Then whether the further drop of consumption is of the order of 10 per cent or of the order of 5 per cent there is no reason for the output of capital goods to increase above zero, since in either case the plant is still too large. The decline in the rate of decline of consumption does not produce a turning-point in the output of capital goods, as did the decline in the rate of increase.

Thirdly, as already mentioned apropos of Mr Kalecki, there are a number of forces influencing decisions about capital outlay other than the physical pressure of consumption demand.

I suspect that Hicks in his treatment has done most of what expertise and ingenuity can do to reduce these complications to conceptually manageable form; whether anyone can make them econometrically as well as conceptually manageable I do not know. My own difficulty about his treatment, which he has mentioned (p. 40, n.) but which I am not sure that he has fully met, is that when he comes to introducing lags, his lag seems to me the wrong way round, or partly so. He makes the instalment of new plant *follow* the relevant increase in output, whereas it seems to me that what happens is that *demand* increases, then new plant is installed, and then, after a period of gestation which may be prolonged and whose length is of great importance to the working of the cycle, comes the birth of the increase in output.

It is noteworthy that Tinbergen rejects the acceleration principle from his system altogether, making profits, or perhaps also the rate of increase of profits, the sole avenue of transmission for the effect of demand for consumption goods on demand for capital goods; and so, I think, does Kaldor. That also I venture to find unsatisfactory; for if we are concerned less with building models than with understanding causes, and obstacles in the way of cure, I do not see, as I have already said, how we can refuse to allow the root idea of the acceleration principle to bulk pretty largely in our thoughts, however unruly it proves as an element in a model.

VIII

THE TRADE CYCLE: GENERAL POLICY

In turning to the discussion of policy in respect of cyclical fluctuation, I must draw particular attention to the fact that my analysis is limited to a closed system. With an open system there may well be complications due to the difficulty of reconciling, or choosing or compromising between, conflicting objectives. In a weak debtor country, an expansionist policy in depression which might be right for internal reasons may have to be ruled out because of its possibly disastrous effect on the balance of payments. Or again, as the American Authorities found in 1927–9, an expansionist policy undertaken by a strong creditor country, partly at least in order to ease the international situation, may have unfortunate inflammatory effects at home. It may be virtually impossible to act rightly both from the internal and external point of view.

Further, in an open system the sharp distinction which I shall draw at certain points of my argument between consumption goods and capital goods becomes blurred, since an improvement in the balance of payments on current account has in certain respects the same effect as an increase in capital outlay at home, and the former may be secured by an increase in the output not of capital goods but of certain types of consumption goods: while, conversely, it is largely by the production of capital goods for export that we earn our daily bread instead of producing it for ourselves.

You will be hearing much about all this from others, and in my treatment I must stick to the assumption that we are dealing with a closed system, or, which comes to much the same thing, that the danger of our country getting out of step with others is being looked after effectively by some kind of international action.

This being understood, in discussing policy in respect of cyclical fluctuation, I shall reverse the order and start in pronounced depression. This of course involves the assumption that past policy has not been so successful as to prevent depression from occurring. If you feel this to be unduly pessimistic, you must take what I say as referring to what *should have* been done in the past!

In pronounced depression, the prima facie duty of the Monetary Authority in a free enterprise economy is to promote the re-expansion of the stream of money income, endeavouring to counteract the increase in K by expansion of M, and bringing down the rates of interest even below the relatively low level to which, as I have argued earlier, they will have fallen naturally during the process of contraction and which may themselves be below that 'natural' rate which would have kept a stable economy stable, but which, since fluctuation has set in, has disappeared as a guide to immediate policy.[1] If there is much unused capacity of plant and labour, and large unsold stocks of raw materials etc., the effect of such an expansionist policy may be manifested at first chiefly in an increase of output, and hardly at all in a rise of prices. But even when prices begin to rise, so that there is some redistribution of income against rentiers and employed workpeople and in favour of entrepreneurs as compared with the position at the bottom of the slump, it does not of course follow that the policy of expansion is wrong or should be suspended. If we choose to say that it involves the making of 'forced levies' in the sense that those with fixed or sticky money incomes are getting less real income than they expected in the light of their experience in the recent past, we should add that under such conditions it seems to be in the social interest that 'forced levies' should be imposed

[1] See my *Essays*, pp. 88–9.

at least until some position of 'normality' in the relative rewards of the factors of production, corresponding to their long-run expectations, is once more restored. Nor, I think, can it be plausibly held that the expansionist policy should be called off as soon as there is any rise in money wage rates, though that is the inference which might be drawn from the definition of 'involuntary un-employment' adopted by Keynes in his *General Theory*. That definition has always seemed to me confusing and paradoxical; for you will recollect that, according to it, a worker is only held to have been 'involuntarily unem-ployed' if he will accept a fall in real wages which comes in the guise of rising prices though he would *not* accept one which comes in the guise of falling money wages; i.e. if, after finding employment, he does not react, by de-manding higher money wages, to a fall in real wages which has occurred as a result of rising prices.

For reasons already given, it may however prove very difficult to promote even a moderate degree of expansion by purely monetary means. The public may prefer, if confidence is lacking, to keep newly created money idle rather than use it; and the banks may take the same line about reserves created for their benefit by the Central Bank. As already explained, the long-term rate of interest may lag seriously behind the short-term rate in its fall; and even if gilt-edged rates are successfully brought down, the capital market may prove very imperfect, so that the effective rate to industrial borrowers, or some of them, remains relatively high. And, again if confidence is lacking, the response of borrowers to any fall either of long-term or short-term rates may be disappointing. In the face of pronounced depression, 'cheap money' can create con-ditions favourable for a recovery of enterprise, but it cannot necessarily do much more.

There is thus a strong case for bringing other instru-ments of policy, especially the instrument of Public

Finance, to the aid of the Monetary Authorities. The most obvious suggestion is that governments, Central and Local, as well as semi-public concerns such as railways, utilities and so forth, should organise their programmes of construction ahead, so as to be ready to come on to the markets for investable funds, for materials and for labour when they are slack, thus fitting their demands into the interstices left by those of purely private enterprise. Even in countries where private enterprise still predominates, the scope for such policies is clearly greater than it was some fifty or a hundred years ago, since the State is inevitably mixed up anyhow with some of the most prominent and massive forms of capital outlay – roads, electricity, housing, land development. But it presents formidable difficulties of timing, and of making the public demands for labour compensatory in detail, and not merely in gross, for the private demands which have fallen away, unless we are willing to contemplate extensions of State activity which are not only large in scale but in danger, from a long-term point of view, of proving un-balanced – shipbuilding furnishes an obvious problem in this country from this point of view. As long ago as 1926 I found myself writing of the 'once heretical but now perhaps over-respectable' policy of public works; and if you have read Beveridge's treatment of the matter in his *Full Employment in a Free Society*, you will recall that, while in favour of a large programme of public investment for its own sake, he is very sniffy (pp. 158, 262) – over-sniffy, I think – about using it as a compensating factor.

Another type of government action for which there is a good theoretical case is the purchase of stocks of materials – iron, copper, wheat, sugar, cotton, etc. – whose purchase will maintain the incomes of primary producers in the present, and whose release in the future will render possible the building up of working capital and fixed capital by industrialists with less pressure on contemporary abstinence than would otherwise be required. In the inter-war period the practical difficulty of carrying through successfully such schemes of 'valorisation' was rendered very great by the occurrence of long period changes both in demand and technique, involving chronic inexpansibility in the demand for some necessaries, and calling for the permanent supersession rather than the bolstering up of high cost producers. And there is plenty of evidence of the dangers of schemes of this kind making the situation worse by a premature, or over-prolonged, policy of boost; and also of their tendency to become degraded into mere annexes of much more questionable schemes for the planned restriction of output in the interest of high cost producers. Nevertheless they cannot be omitted from any list of possible anti-depression measures. In general, to be effective they would need to be international; and they played a prominent part, under the name of 'buffer stocks', in the blue-prints for a better world to which thought was devoted in the later stages of the war. You will forgive me for repeating a story which percolated to the lower rungs of the Whitehall ladder on which I dwelt, of a meeting at which Cabinet approval was required to some document dealing with this subject, and at which Mr Churchill, who wanted to get on with the war, was heard to growl, 'Butter-scotch, butter-scotch? What's all this about butter-scotch?' So far, at all events, all the 'butter-scotch' talk has produced but one solitary fruit – in the case of tin.

Government borrowing to finance *consumption*, whether through the straight remission of taxation or through the distribution of gifts and subsidies of one kind and another, has become increasingly respectable in the public eye, and therefore increasingly possible to adopt as an anti-depression measure without damaging effects on public confidence and so on the willingness to incur capital outlay. If it does not directly attack depression in the instrumental trades where it is presumably deepest, it can at least do something to check its spread through short-circuiting the operation of the 'multiplier', and lead towards its ultimate removal through setting in motion the 'principle of acceleration'. Apart from tax-reduction, the most obvious channel for this type of deficit financing is of course the payment of unemployment benefit; but it is by no means difficult to think of others as well.

Increased attention, too, has been given in recent years to the possibilities of expanding the stream of money income *without* incurring Government deficits, by modifying the incidence and methods of taxation in such wise as to increase in the aggregate the desire to spend while taking precautions not to impair the incentives to undertake capital outlay. An ingenious scheme of this kind is put forward by Kalecki (Oxford Essays in *The Economics of Full Employment*, No. 2). How much scope there may be for the introduction of such schemes depends of course on the level and distribution of taxation with which you start; but they show a welcome advance on the tendency which was rife in the 1930s, and which is still exhibited by some advocates of 'functional finance' such as Lerner, to treat the indefinite growth of public debt as a matter of no consequence. For the fact that the payment of interest on the public debt is, as is sometimes said, a 'mere transfer' does not of course prevent the taxation required to pay the interest from being a real deterrent to work and enterprise. And any attempt to avert this result by borrowing enough to pay the growing interest on the growing debt is bound, unless we can believe in a very advanced form of the stagnation thesis, to end in an inflationary breakdown.[1]

In general, while there is no doubt that Public Finance has come to stay as *a* main instrument, perhaps *the* main

---

[1] See a salutary comment on Lerner's position by Meade in *E.J.*, March 1945, pp. 62–3.

instrument, of anti-cyclical policy, I feel myself that there are great difficulties about trusting to it as the *sole* instrument, if only because of its relatively inflexible and slow-moving nature. And any attempt to make it pronouncedly more flexible, for instance by entrusting decisions more largely to administrative as opposed to legislative action, may run the risk of impairing its efficiency for other purposes, and especially of damaging that valuable and sensitive plant, the tax-paying habit. There is much to be said for the policy of 'built-in flexibility' which has been preached in recent years by that enlightened body of American industrialists known as the Committee for Economic Development – that is to say, for fixing *rates* of taxation and *programmes* of expenditure which will yield a moderate surplus for debt reduction in normal years, and then permitting the shortfalls of actual tax receipts and the increases of actual disbursements in bad years to exercise their natural effect. Moderate as such a programme may seem to the super-planner, it is both more 'lax' than business interests have ever explicitly advocated in the past and more strict than most governments in recent times, including that of the United States, have in fact found it possible to pursue. I agree, however, with the Douglas Sub-Committee to which I have already alluded, that it may be found to be inadequate to cope with really large movements, and that in the last resort governments which have to take action cannot be bound within the framework of automatically functioning regulators. But I agree, too, with the same Sub-Committee that the shortcomings of *fiscal* policy, however administered, are sufficiently great to make 'an appropriate, vigorous and flexible *monetary* policy' a most desirable adjunct – a view no longer so disreputable in this country as it was during the first few years of the life of this lecture course!

In discussing what is sometimes called 'functional finance'

I have allowed myself to pass out of the phase of deep depression and paint a more general picture. Let us then face explicitly a more difficult question than how to act in deep depression, and put it first in the form in which it has usually presented itself for solution in the past. At what point should the monetary and other measures of expansion just discussed be suspended? It is tempting to reply, as some have done, 'Not until all resources, or at all events all human resources, are fully employed; until that point is reached, "inflation", in any damaging sense, cannot be said to have set in.' But, apart from the behaviour of money wages, to which we will return, that is surely to over-simplify the issue, which is complicated in real life by the emergence of what are now elegantly called bottle-necks in some parts of the economy while in others there is still considerable elasticity of supply. In particular, it is, as it seems to me, to glide over the most important root of the trouble, which is – once more – that in wealthy and progressive economies the installation of, at any rate, some forms of capital equipment is almost bound to be a jerky and discontinuous process, entailing pronounced fluctuation in the output of capital goods and a greater variability of employment in the trades making these than in the consumption trades. Thus at a certain stage in the expansion we may be faced with the alternatives of pressing ahead, in pursuit of full employment, towards a level of activity which we have grave reason, on the basis of past experience, to fear cannot be continuously maintained; or of damping down while there is still a residue of unemployment in the instrumental trades, in the hopes of promoting a partial demobilisation of those trades and a redistribution of resources, in favour of the consumption trades, which will ultimately prove more compatible with stability.

This difficulty seems to be now more clearly realised by some of the apostles of full employment than it used to be. Kalecki, in the Oxford Essay already referred to, rightly says that there is no point in 'piling up unwanted public or private capital equipment', and proposes that at a certain stage in the recovery productive resources should be diverted, by taxation policies stimulating consumption, to the production of consumption goods. But he takes rather lightly the difficulties, bound up with the lumpiness of investment, of *timing* the transfer, as well as the difficulty of effecting it in an economy which, in respect at least of choice of occupation, aims at remaining non-totalitarian, and which indeed, in our case, seems to be showing an increased rather than a diminished reluctance to put pressure on people ever to work in unaccustomed localities or jobs. On the other hand, it may well be that Kalecki and other devotees of the 'stagnation thesis' overestimate the need for artificial stimuli to the 'propensity to consume' in order to induce a gradual change in the relative size of the consumption goods and capital goods industries, if in the interest of stability that is what is desired; for in so far as an expansion has been carried out by *repressing* that propensity through what we have called 'forced levies' or other expedients for enforcing abstinence, then merely letting the propensity to consume have its head might do a good deal to stimulate occupational transfer.

What it seems to come to is that how high we set our sights as regards the permanent abolition of unemployment depends partly, as it always has, on a choice between the conflicting claims of Progress and Stability, and partly on our readiness to use drastic measures, or alternatively our skill in devising milder measures, to promote the occupational mobility of labour. On p. 327 of the *General Theory* you will find that I am subjected by Keynes to mild reproof for having in the 1930s set my sights too low. That may or may not have been; certainly I thought – apart from all my criticisms of detail – that the general tenor of that famous book, with its dramatisation of the contrast between general or mass unemployment on the one hand and 'full employment' – a phrase I have always mistrusted – on the other, over-simplified the problem of objectives as it then presented itself. Nor do I believe that war and the post-war reconstruction boom have solved it for us, or even for those more fortunate countries who are exempt, as we are not, from the shadow of that quite different kind of unemployment which is associated with lack of material on which to set men to work. What war and reconstruction boom and later rearmament boom have done is to cause the problem to appear in a new form, namely, not how close an approximation to absolutely full employment should we aim at reaching, but how large a retreat from absolutely full employment – *over*-employment, as some of us have not hesitated to describe it – should we tolerate occurring. Politically and psychologically, the problem in its new form is even more delicate and explosive, since men hate to lose what they have once had more than to fail to attain what they have never had. Economically, it is in essence the same old problem as before, – namely, how much slack does a modern economy require in order to avoid ossification of its industrial structure and a progressive undermining of its standard of value? Not so much, it may be, as used to be supposed; but more, I think economists must have the courage to say, even if the security of their own job renders it repugnant to them to say it – more than is found existing at the apex of a post-war reconstruction boom, fed by evanescent backlogs of demand and watered, wisely or not, by streams of cheap money. And if it *is* desired to damp down the hyper-inflation, at the cost of some temporary unemployment, experience seems to show that there are definite limits to the efficacy of budgetary action, in the form of very high taxation, as an instrument for doing so, since it is bound to fall largely on saving rather than on consumption expenditure, and so, given the magnitude of inflexible investment programmes, to make the situation no less, or scarcely less, inflationary than it would otherwise have been. If one *does* attach importance to stability, it looks as if one must be prepared to pay the price in damping down somewhat the rate of progress which one aims to achieve.

PRELUDE TO CHAPTER IX
References on Wages and Employment

KEYNES. *General Theory*, p. 13 (first thoughts).[1]
ch. 19 (second thoughts).
HABERLER. *Prosperity and Depression*, pp. 239–44, 395–405, 491–503.
—— In *The New Economics*, p. 172.
PIGOU. *Employment and Equilibrium* (second edition), II, 6.
—— *Lapses from Full Employment*, pp. 22–5, 51.
TOBIN. In *The New Economics*, pp. 572–90.
VINER. *Q.J.E.*, November 1936, pp. 160–3.
BEVERIDGE. *Full Employment in a Free Society*, pp. 97, 182.
LANGE. *Price Flexibility and Employment*, ch. IV, and review by Harrod in *E.J.*, March 1946.

---

[1] 'There may exist no expedient by which labour as a whole can reduce its *real* wage to a given figure by making revised *money* bargains with the entrepreneurs. *This will be our contention.*' (My italics in last sentence. – D.H.R.)

IX

THE TRADE CYCLE: WAGE POLICY

There remains one more element of trade cycle policy to be discussed, and that the thorniest of all, namely wage policy. In our discussion of 'monetary equilibrium' and the action necessary to preserve or restore it, we have in effect laid down that the Authorities should act on the other elements of the problem in the light of their knowledge that money wages, either per hour or perhaps under some conditions per unit of output, are in fact relatively sticky. But that does not dispose of the question. How far, if these other elements prove intractable, could greater flexibility in money wage rates promote stability of employment?

I can perhaps best introduce a discussion of this problem by means of a little dialogue between an Advocate and an Opponent of general wage reduction as a remedy for unemployment in the position of temporary under-employment quasi-equilibrium reached at the bottom of an ordinary trade depression. The Advocate starts off:

A. 'If the stream of money demand is deficient, that must mean that it is deficient relatively to the existing money wage rate. If the money wage rate were lower, a given stream of money demand would obviously go further and employ more people.'

O. 'Yes, but wages are an income as well as a cost. The reduction of the money wage rate will itself diminish the stream of money demand, so that prices will fall as much as wage rates and we are no further on – the *real* wage rate is unchanged, and the attempt of the workpeople to accept a reduction thereof has been thwarted.'[1]

---

[1] Cf. Keynes, 'first thoughts', in list of references, p. 123.

A. 'No; for wages are not the only sort of income, and non-wage money income will be initially unchanged. Hence total money income will fall initially in a smaller proportion than the wage bill, and prices therefore will fall in a smaller proportion than the money wage rate. Price will stand in excess of marginal cost, and entrepreneurs therefore will have an inducement to expand output till these two are equal again.'

O. 'No: for non-wage-earners, finding their real incomes increased by the fall in prices, will want to save part of the increase, so that if entrepreneurs try to increase output they will find themselves making losses till they reduce it again to the old level.'

A. 'Ah! the capital market, assisted if necessary by the Monetary Authority, will look after that. I assume, of course, that the Authority is not so stupid or spiteful as to pursue a policy in opposition to the wage policy which is being followed, but does its best, if there is an increase in thrift, to canalise it into capital outlay.'

O. 'Well, I've already told you that's a very slow and uncertain process, partly because money gets held up in the liquidity trap, and partly because capital outlay doesn't respond at all readily to a fall in interest rates. Still, I would agree that there *is* a route from wage reduction to increased employment through increased ease of monetary conditions and consequent stimulus to capital outlay; but I say that this means that you have achieved nothing by the wage reduction that you couldn't have achieved through an expansionist monetary policy, which would have been much less painful to all concerned.'

I will suspend the dialogue at this point to remark that it was on this sort of basis that, after a difficult discussion in the *Economic Journal* in 1937–8, a concordat was reached between Pigou and Kaldor for a particular model with zero capital outlay, and that the result was later generalised by Pigou in his *Employment and Equilibrium*. There it is established, subject to certain complications about monopoly, that, as between two situations similar in other relevant respects, in that situation in which the money wage rate is lower, money income and the rate of interest will also be lower and employment will be higher, unless indeed monetary policy is of a kind designed to prevent this result by deliberately keeping up the rate of interest. (Let me warn you in passing that in the listed passage by Beveridge (p. 97) the Pigou-Kaldor concordat is alluded to in words from which the guileless reader would, I think, never guess that what it established was not that a wage reduction *wouldn't* increase employment in the assumed circumstances but that it *would*!)

Now, in the light of this provisional conclusion, let us look back at the situation which Pigou called Lord Keynes's Day of Judgment – the situation in which, with a glut of capital equipment, the rate of interest has fallen to zero, or perhaps a little above zero, but the desire to save still persists, so that the liquidity trap is operating at full strength and money income is, to start with, progressively declining. If money wages are rigid, there will obviously be great and increasing unemployment. What happens if they are completely flexible, and flexible without lag, – for instance if, in the extreme case, they are linked by an instantaneous sliding scale to the money demand for the product? To isolate the issue, let us assume that wages are the only relevant costs, so that the entrepreneur's actions are not affected by the rigidity, for instance, of old debt charges fixed in money. The Keynesian view is, I think, that even on this assumption the flexibility of money wages would not prevent the emergence of mass unemployment, which would grow and grow until, as a result of the consequent reduction in real income and therefore in saving, a stable position is again reached at a very low level both of money income and of employment. Now that does not seem to be correct. On the contrary, in the extreme case supposed, it seems that no unemployment need ever develop at all, since at every moment the money cost of the worker's services is being reduced in exact proportion to the money value of his work. It would be a very uncomfortable world, but it would not be, on our present assumptions, a world with unemployment. Let us therefore go on to assume, more plausibly, that as a result of an initial lag in wage reduction behind the fall in aggregate money demand, *some* unemployment has already developed, but that thereafter money wage rates and aggregate money demand fall *pari passu*. In this case the fall in money wage rates will prima facie be powerless to cure the unemployment which has already developed, since the route by which it has been agreed that in other circumstances it might do so, viz. the route through the rate of interest, is now definitely closed. But, as before, there is no need for unemployment to get any *worse*; i.e. if wages are perfectly flexible, even though with a lag, the Keynesian position of mass unemployment equilibrium will never be reached.

Will there then be no check to the progressive fall in money income? Yes, on the lines of what I will still venture to call ordinary monetary theory, there will be. For as a result of the progressive fall in prices there will be a progressive increase in the real value of the community's money stock, which will come to bear a larger and larger proportion to its real income; and in accordance with ordinary monetary doctrine the community will not sit down under this, but will seek to restore K to its old level. If capital outlay is ruled out by the fall in the rate of return on real investment to zero, the community will spend on consumption goods. In other words it is a mistake to suppose that the function linking consumption to real income must be taken as a fixed factor in the situation. What people desire to spend on consumption depends on their capital position – especially their liquid capital position – as well as on their income; and since, in the case supposed, their liquid capital position is rapidly improving in real terms, it is natural to suppose that sooner or later they will start spending on a scale sufficient to restore equilibrium, if not with no unemployment at all, at any rate with employment far above the level portrayed in the Keynesian picture.

This argument has been set out in various of his later works, especially *Lapses from Full Employment* (pp. 22–5), by Pigou, who has thus, as it seems to me, in respect of this highly hypothetical case of the completely capital-glutted economy, delivered himself from the toils of the Pigou-Kaldor concordat, whose validity depends on the assumption of a fixed income-consumption function. But the argument has also been invoked by other writers as one among other reasons why wage reduction may be expected to contribute to the economic system's powers of recuperation from an ordinary depression. See the listed passages by Haberler and Tobin; the argument is also countenanced, though not very warmly, by Lange (listed chapter), for which he was taken to task in a review by Harrod, who, so far as I can see, simply rejects the argument without giving any reason for doing so. To me it appears to be in principle entirely sound, and a very good illustration of the way in which the old Cambridge equation, with its emphasis on K, can profitably be used to check conclusions based on the tacit assumption of an immutable income-consumption function.

But that is not all. There is another assumption underlying the Pigou-Kaldor concordat which is often unnoticed, but which, when looked into, appears to be highly questionable. This is that the schedule exhibiting the amount of real capital outlay as a function of the rate of interest is unchanged by the wage reduction – that in Keynes's language what is given is the schedule of marginal efficiency of capital *in terms of wage units*. That is to say, it is assumed that when the reduction of money wage rates occurs entrepreneurs immediately conclude that all future net money yields of instruments will shrink in direct proportion to the fall which has occurred in the money labour cost of constructing and operating them; and this seems to be a pretty queer assumption. Once we allow ourselves to take a more dynamic view, the door is open to the common-sense arguments in favour of the efficacy of wage reduction which were adduced by Viner in his original review of the *General Theory* (see list of references). The lag, so Viner argues, between the wage reduction and any consequent decline in sales will suffice to give entrepreneurs the *inducement* to set in hand all sorts of postponable expenditure on equipment, etc., which they have perforce been postponing during depression, and will also increase their *power* of acting in this way by improving their credit status. To the extent that this is true, a policy of wage reduction will be more likely to eventuate in definite concrete acts of capital outlay than will a policy of easy money, and may truthfully be said to act on employment quite directly, and not through the rate of interest.

Let it be granted, however, that once we begin to talk in terms of plans and expectations anything *may* happen. Thus it is common ground that if the wage reduction is expected to be followed shortly by further reductions, entrepreneurs may hold off for the time being from the hire of additional labour; all this means is that, as with any other price, a fairly large clean cut is likely to be more efficacious in stimulating demand than a series of nibbles. And the dangers, such as they are, of wage flexibility promoting excessive instability of the whole price system can be countered, as Haberler points out (p. 503), by combining wage reduction with an expansionary policy in other directions – public works or what not – as was done in Australia in the 1930s.[1]

Pigou has presented what seems to me pretty persuasive historical evidence to the effect that the willingness of British labour to accept reductions helped to keep *average* unemployment over the trade cycle not of course at zero but at a pretty steady 5 per cent in the sixty years before 1914; while the greater rigidity of wages in the inter-war period due to the existence of unemployment insurance was associated with much greater unemployment. It may be true, as is often said, that a general wage reduction in time of depression would now be politically impossible here, though in point of fact, under sufficient stress, politically impossible things sometimes tend to happen. But one ought to try to keep economic analysis and political judgment apart as long as possible, and I cannot help thinking that in this matter there has been a particular tendency to link them up prematurely. It is one thing to say that for political reasons wage reductions in time of depression have become impossible; it is quite another thing to claim that by this change the economic system has gained in stability or recuperative power.

I turn now to the companion problem of the effect, if any, of a *rise* in money wage rates in checking the growth of employment or causing it to decline. So long as we are content to deal in terms of comparative statics, the picture is of course one of complete symmetry. In Pigou's model the economy with a higher money wage rate is the economy which has also a higher total of money income, a higher rate of interest and a lower level of employment. And this model, be it remembered, while it is a short-

---

[1] Australasian writers, by the way, have given a good deal of attention to this subject, not always with agreement. Thus Isles (*Wages Policy and the Price Level*, p. 162) and Walker (*Australia in the World Depression*, p. 187), each writing after a period of exposure to the theoretical blasts of Cambridge, concluded, the one, that wage reductions are more likely to do good at the very beginning of a recession, the other, when the bottom has already been passed!

period one in the sense that it does not take account of the consequences of capital growth, is a *stable* one; that is to say, an economy which is 'classical' in the sense that monetary equilibrium is being preserved is by no means necessarily an economy with full employment if the Trade Unions choose to make it otherwise. This we took full account of last term, in our 'non-monetary' discussion of the theory of wages, in which it was emphasised that unemployment will occur if people demand more than they are worth.

When we turn to a fluctuating system, in which even a temporary 'monetary equilibrium' is not established, there is more to be said. In the first place, as Pigou has argued clearly, though not I think sufficiently prominently (*Lapses*, p. 51), the money wage rate is, in the modern political atmosphere, more easily shifted upwards than downwards in response to swings of money demand; so that its *average* level over a cycle is more nearly adapted to the boom level of money demand than to the slump level. From this an important consequence follows. Suppose means could be found to stabilise the level of money demand; then there seems good reason to hope that the money wage rate would become more closely adapted to the new stable level of demand than the previous *average* rate was to the previous *average* level of demand, and the amount of unemployment therefore would be less than the previous average amount. This is quite a separate point from the one I made in an earlier connection, namely that a successful stabilisation of demand should promote ultimately a migration of labour from the more fluctuating instrumental industries to the less fluctuating consumption industries. Both points were completely missed by Beveridge and his advisers, who, in pursuance of their determination to disparage the policy of stabilisation of demand as being too unambitious an aim, assume that it would simply mean the redistribution of a given amount of unemployment through time without any reduction of the total as measured over a stretch of years (*F.E. in a F.S.*, p. 182; Burckhardt in Oxford *Essays*, p. 15).

Secondly, it seems much more likely that we shall find a lack of harmony between monetary policy and wage policy in boom than in depression. For, to judge from the experience of recent years, it is much more likely that modern Monetary Authorities will carry on with a cheap money policy when workpeople are exacting rises in money wage rates than that they would ever pursue a dear money policy when workpeople were being so helpful as to accept a reduction in money wage rates. In the extreme case, i.e. if the Monetary Authority simply dishes out enough money to implement whatever money wage bill Mr John Lewis, or whoever it may be, regards as appropriate, we get a situation in some respects parallel but opposite to that which we examined under the name of the Day of Judgment. Just as there, the interest mechanism having jammed, it seemed as if we might get the money wage rate slipping down and down without any beneficial effect on employment, at any rate until we got to the final remedy of the Consumers' Spree, so here it seems as if we might get the money wage rate slipping up and up without any adverse effect on employment, or therefore any compulsion being exercised on Mr John Lewis, or whoever it may be, to moderate his demands. We reach therefore a curious result, which I shall make no apology for stating in terms in which I have already stated it in print. 'In the bad old unenlightened days, it was possible for the detached observer to welcome the rises in money wage rates which took place during the later phases of a trade expansion – to welcome them not only on distributional grounds but because, even if they prevented so close an approach to absolutely full employment as might otherwise have been achieved, they could be regarded as working, in conjunction with a firm monetary policy, to encroach on windfall profits and so to keep the ambitions and optimism of entrepreneurs within bounds. But in the new enlightened days it becomes necessary to regard such rises in money wage rates with apprehension, not because they carry a threat of unemployment but precisely because they do not, or rather because the unemployment of which they carry a threat is not the relatively mild type usually associated with a trade recession, but the much more frightening type associated with a breakdown of the standard of value or, in the case of a country dependent on imported raw materials, with a dearth of material on which to set men to work' (*Three Banks Review*, March 1949, reprinted in *Utility and All That*, p. 92).

And so, to do them justice, we find Beveridge and some other prophets of 'full employment' as ready as any classical economist to lecture the Trade Unions on the virtues of moderation and the need to evolve an overall wages policy. Whether that is what Trade Unions are for, and whether their mentors' chances of being listened to have been increased by years of optimistic talk about the 'humbug of finance' and 'investment breeding its own saving' is another matter, or rather two other matters. Some of us in recent years have felt bound to go on insisting that in the last resort the stoppage of inflation is the duty not of Trade Unions but of Governments, and that unless the Monetary Authority plays *its* part by catching and keeping firm hold of the supply of money, these efforts at what I have called stroking the ears of the Trade Union movement are not likely to be very successful.

But if once we could assume some sort of stability in the supply of money, then the two holes which I have picked in the Keynesian theory in its application to wage reductions would become relevant also in respect of wage advances. First, the income-consumption function cannot be taken to be invariable in the face of an upward-sliding price and wage level any more than in the case of a downward-sliding one. In the face of a progressive rise of prices and reduction in the real value of money stocks, K would reassert itself, people would try to restore the real value of their money balances, and a Consumers' Strike would take, as a limiting factor on the rise of total money income, the same sort of place as we assigned to the Consumers' Spree in limiting its fall. Secondly, the Keynesian assumption that the marginal efficiency of capital, or whatever you like to call it, is given in terms of wage units, and so slides upwards indefinitely with the level of money wage rates, would become patently invalid over a sufficiently large field of industry to cause a contraction in the demand for labour in some at least of the construction trades, and so set in motion a cumulative downward process of the usual kind. Whether that is an optimistic or a pessimistic conclusion I do not know. It means that we *needn't* let the wild horses of runaway inflation carry us to perdition unless we choose. But it means, too, that it may be very difficult to pull them up in mid-career without suffering something of a jolt and a shock. How great that shock and jolt need be, and in particular how largely it takes the form of unemployment, *would* depend largely on the wage policy of Trade Unions; and that is when good leadership from inside, and even ear-stroking from outside, would have a genuine part to play, namely in inducing the Trade Unions to take their share of the medicine of stabilisation in the form of abstention from pressure for wage advances rather than in the form of unemployment.

What are the chances of a happy issue of this kind in this country at the present time? Up to a few months ago there seemed good reason for being fairly optimistic. It is true that neither the Government's ear-stroking endeavours nor the credit squeeze had deterred the great

Trade Unions from putting forward in the autumn claims for wage advances on the usual high, wide and handsome scale; but the 10 per cent claim of the engineering and shipbuilding workers had come up against a brick wall, arbitration had substituted 3 per cent for the locomotive men's 10 per cent and been accepted, a similar offer to the other railwaymen was under arbitration, and similar arrangements in other industries were being arrived at. It looked as though, even if that brick wall in engineering and shipbuilding should give way a little, before or after stoppage of work, the general pattern of wage advances for the year would not exceed 3 per cent. Perhaps that was really too much, at the end of a year in which there had been almost no increase at all in the total national product. But if this kind of result could have been achieved, it would, I think, in all the circumstances, have been fairly convincing evidence, first that there *is* a clear link between monetary policy and the money wage level, and secondly that it doesn't require either tremendous sermonisings or horrifying levels of unemployment to make that link effective, but only a reasonable amount of courage on the part of politicians and a reasonable amount of enlightened self-interest on the part of the leaders of organised labour.

But we optimists had reckoned without several things. First, that the conflict in shipbuilding, a relatively small and homogeneous industry which, whatever its other troubles, is suffering from no dearth of orders, would on this occasion be brought to a head, against the usual custom, in advance of that in its big, sprawling, much patchier brother, the so-called industry of engineering, and hence that the settlement obtained in shipbuilding would be likely to form a pattern for that in engineering rather than the other way round. Secondly, that there exists in the heart of the economy one industry, railway transport, which, for good reasons or bad, has been so

completely exempted from ordinary financial responsibilities that in its wage policy it is a law unto itself; and this
industry felt itself constrained under the imminent men-
ace of a strike, to go back on the majority decision
of its own arbitral body and outbid its own previous
offers, uniting with the shipbuilders to hold out 5 per cent
instead of 3 per cent as this year's price of peace. Thirdly,
the complex body which we call the Government contains
as one element a very efficient and high-minded organ
called the Ministry of Labour, whose prestige is bound
up with the doctrines that the Government has got
nothing to do with wages and that any settlement of a
dispute is better than a stoppage of work, however much
the terms of settlement may conflict with the aims of other
branches of Government policy. Finally, just at this
juncture the Monetary Authorities found what seemed to
them good technical reasons for making one cut in Bank
rate and raising strong hopes of another – actions which,
however carefully explained away, helped to precipitate a
renewed boom in ordinary shares which was scarcely
helpful towards inculcating the need for wage restraint.

Exactly how all this will work out on the 1957–8 wage
level and price level it is still too early to say; but I am
afraid I am not in a position to assure you, as I should like
to be, that monetary policy has killed the wage inflation
dead, and that without any serious damage to employment.

I must, however, after this rather long topical digres-
sion, return to the main thread of my argument. One way
and another, I submit (in this concurring with Howard
Ellis's judgment, listed work, p. 475), there is not much
left of the simpliste Keynesian doctrine that the level of
employment does not depend at all on the level of money
wage rates. Given a sufficiently firm and flexible monetary
policy, which is not being sabotaged by other organs of
Government, I suggest that it *does* largely so depend.
And I will end my main argument by pointing out that

one of the weapons which we have found most serviceable
in probing into the entrails of the Keynesian doctrine is
that 'ancient ceremony' with whose observance we began
the term, and which I will now write up one more in its
most provocative form:

$$\frac{1}{P} = \frac{KR}{M}$$

– the value of money depends on the conditions of demand
for it and on the quantity of it which is permitted to exist.

Now for some final reflections, by way of attempt to pull
the whole story together. In the October term we were
studying a steady system, this term we have been studying
an unsteady one. In that term the centre of our interest was
the allocation of productive resources between different
uses, in this term it has been the degree to which they are
being used at all. Economics has always consisted of these
two branches, though the names for them have varied.
One used to contrast the theory of value with the theory of
money and the trade cycle; latterly it has become fashionable to talk about micro-economics and macro-economics;
and sometimes in the controversies of recent years the
contrast has been crudely dramatised into an opposition
between 'classical economics' and 'Keynesian economics'.
    What is the relation between these two branches of
study? Obviously they are complementary, and the
economist must attend to both of them and try to effect
his own synthesis between them. The theory of money or
employment or whatever you like to call it does not
supersede the theory of value, though it modifies its
operation – movements of the general level of prices
usually involve a dispersion of individual prices, movements of general activity affect different industries in
different degrees.
    In time of deep depression it is right to remember that
it is better to produce something – better perhaps even to

dig holes in the ground – than to produce nothing at all. Conversely, in times of high inflation it is right to remember that it is better to cut down something than to cut down nothing. But even in a depression it is better to produce some things than others; and even in an inflation it is better to cut down some things than others. Preoccupation with movements of the whole system must not lead us to shut our eyes to the operation of the laws of relative value, or suppose that they have become obsolete.

Well, that brings me to an end. When I concluded, eleven years ago, my first endeavour to deliver this particular course, I told my audience that they had been the dogs whose fate it had been to have tried on them a first attempt to set in order what can usefully be said about the 'Principles of Economics' in this confusing and transitional world in which we are all called on to live. I thanked them for being very kind and helpful dogs, and told them I hoped their successors might profit from the blunders and faults of proportion which they had had to put up with.

I'm afraid that hope has not been completely fulfilled. One still makes blunders, especially if one has a piece of chalk in the hand, and one still finds it difficult to see things and present them in the right order and proportion. And though I have continued to get help and stimulus from each successive pack of dogs, there will be, I am afraid, no further improvement: for I have now – in point of fact this very day – reached the age of 67 at which dons become officially gaga, and this course of lectures will not be given again, though I would not put it past it to get em bodied in due time in a little book. Meanwhile let me just say this. Some of the things I have had to say have not, I suspect, seemed as unfamiliar and shocking to you as they did to your predecessors of six or seven years ago. But if I *have* at times seemed to some at least of you to have been unduly negative and critical of some modern trends in thought and policy, I can only reply in the words I have used at the end of the 1948 edition of my little book on *Money* — that I hope you'll put it down 'not to any lack of desire that the Muse of Economic Theory should serve as the handmaid of all good causes, but only to a certain jealousy on her behalf lest, in attempting to atone for real or fancied misdeeds in the past, she should incur fresh discredit by leading people up the garden path'.

ANNEXE

I

STABILITY AND PROGRESS: THE RICHER COUNTRIES' PROBLEM[1]

Those who have planned this series of addresses have made a heroic attempt to divide the indivisible. To Professor Viner and myself has been allotted the general question – no small one – of Stability and Progress; to Professors Perroux, Haberler and Lundberg some of its particular aspects. Further, somewhat as Pope Alexander VI divided the New World between Spain and Portugal, so our officers have divided the *whole* world between Viner and myself. I yield to him Asia, Africa and South America more whole-heartedly than ever Octavian surrendered the gorgeous East to Antony, and I do not think I shall often be found trespassing in his orchard. But to my other three colleagues I offer my apologies if I find that I cannot discharge my task, even within the limits of my inadequate knowledge and understanding, without some mention of technology, of money, of international trade.

There is a further difficulty. Mine is a very wide and far-flung empire – 'realms and islands are as plates dropped from my pocket'. What they have in common is to be richer rather than poorer; but they differ among themselves in many ways, and it is not easy to frame general propositions which apply to them all. It seems to me that for my purposes two of these causes of difference are outstanding. First, some of my countries are centrally ruled and planned to such a degree that their rulers may, for all I know, be in a position to achieve, at all events in

[1] An address delivered at the Congress of the International Economic Association in Rome, September 1956, and printed in its Proceedings (Macmillan & Co., 1958).

the economic sphere, precisely what they want to achieve; but in others, while the visitor to them may hear a great deal about objectives, policies and even plans, it is of the essence of the matter that these projects are both partial and uncertain of fulfilment. Secondly, in some of my countries policies and plans can be framed with very little regard to external influences; in others these external influences are of dominant importance. Of this second dichotomy, which is a matter of degree, I shall try to take some account; but in the face of the first, even if it be also really a matter of degree, I shall take evasive action. In other words I shall not attempt to extend my analysis beyond the border of what most of us, whether justifiably or not, are in the habit of labelling the free world. Within that limitation, then, here goes.

I

On looking up one of the recognised English authorities, I found, as I expected, that the fundamental question about progress with which any country is faced had been posed long ago with exquisite simplicity.[1] 'The Caterpillar was the first to speak. "What size do you want to be?" it asked.' Alice's reply, 'Oh, I'm not particular as to size, only one doesn't like changing so often, you know,' while natural enough in view of the trying experiences through which she had just passed, will not really do; and the Caterpillar's blunt retort, 'I *don't* know,' was, in my opinion, fully justified. For it would seem that a country, richer or poorer, *ought* to try to form an idea what size it wants to be – more precisely at what rate, if any, it desires to see its national income growing, and what proportion of its current income it should save and invest in order to achieve the desired result. Yet it is extremely hard to formulate any rational grounds for arriving at a decision. As is well known, another authority, Frank Ramsey,[2]

[1] *Alice's Adventures in Wonderland*, Macmillan, People's Edition, p. 61.
[2] 'A Mathematical Theory of Saving', *Economic Journal*, December 1928.

some thirty years ago attempted to give, for a completely single-minded community constant in numbers, a solution framed in terms of the ordinary economic calculus of utilities and disutilities. If such a community is completely indifferent emotionally between the present and the future, the answer, you will remember, depends entirely on the function relating utility to consumption and on the maximum possible utility, conceived as finite, derivable from consumption. If on the other hand the community is not immune from feelings of time preference, then the solution depends also on the strength of this time preference, expressed as a rate of discount, and on the rate of return obtainable from the investment of savings. Professor Stone has shown recently[1] how the method can be adapted to the case of a growing population. But, as Ramsey warns us, these simplified solutions abstract from many difficulties rooted in the uncertainty of human affairs – in those possibilities of technological upheaval and of massed destruction of capital from which even the most totalitarian society is not exempt.

Further, not everyone, I think, will be convinced by Ramsey's idea of finite Bliss – a ceiling on the utility conceivably derivable from consumption. I have heard it argued that the ceiling is essentially a movable one, receding always as you think you have made an approach towards it. Further again, drastic revision of the solution seems to be required when we pass from the well-drilled, like-minded community to a society of ordinary men, each not only with his personal hopes and fears and myopias but with his well-founded certainty of individual deterioration and demise. For the Ramseyan equation depends on the assumption that the economic operator whose utility function is involved realises that its income and its consumption are going continually to increase. But the ordinary man is well aware that on retirement his indi-

[1] 'Misery and Bliss', *Economia Internazionale*, No. 1, 1955.

vidual income is going to fall with a bump, and that at
death his individual consumption is going to cease; and
it seems to be not only inevitable but reasonable that his
savings policy, while influenced also by regard for his
heirs, should partly be governed by that knowledge.

One way and another, then, I am not sanguine about
the possibility of determining the right rate of growth for
a country by mathematical formulae. And the difficulty is
increased when we remember, as Professor Devons has
recently in a most penetrating paper[1] reminded us, that
the sacrifices necessary to achieve growth consist not
merely in passive abstinence from consumption but in
something which is much harder to evaluate mathematic-
ally, namely consent to being disturbed in established
routines of life and work. I do not find it possible to go
further than attempting to list some of the considerations
which a citizen of one of my countries – whether or not
he be also a cabinet minister – might do well to bear in
mind in attempting to arrive at a hunch whether the
proportion of his country's income which is being set aside
in the interests of growth is excessive or defective or just
about right – it being then for further discussion whether
the excess or defect is so great as to justify endeavours to
reduce it by propaganda, by compulsion, by modifying
the distribution of income, or in any other way.

(1) The first and most obvious consideration is the
probable behaviour of population, in respect both of total
numbers and of all the subsidiary complications of age
distribution. Here of course we are in danger of going
round in circles; capital formation may be about right
relatively to body formation, but is body formation itself
on the right scale? If I were dealing with Viner's half of
the world, I should have to say a great deal about this;
and I am not saying that in my half, too, there should not
be policies designed to influence the rate of growth of

[1] *Lloyds Bank Review*, October 1955.

numbers. In Britain a Royal Commission assured us in 1949 that the existing size of the population was about right, and its members were fertile in devices for eliciting that missing one-seventh of a child per completed family which was needed to keep the population stable in the long run. Holland is anxious about her high birth rate as a source of pressure on the standard of life, the United States, apparently, exultant about hers as a guarantee of the buoyancy of effective demand. Perhaps we should all agree that, if only we knew how to get it, what would really be most convenient is a population which is always growing but never getting any bigger. Meanwhile I do not venture beyond the platitude that our views on the right scale of capital formation must be greatly coloured by what is in fact happening or thought likely to happen to numbers.

(2) The second factor which I think might go towards the formation of our hunch – and here too I acknowledge a debt to Professor Devons – is consideration of the *kinds* of improvement in its standard of life which are open to a population which is already by hypothesis fairly well off. We talk glibly of doubling or trebling the standard of life in so many years, but what in detail do we conceive of that as implying? Throughout much of human history two of the most important marks distinguishing the rich man from the poor man have been that he could occupy more *space* and that he could command more personal *service*. But these are precisely the two advantages which it is most difficult to generalise throughout large and urbanised populations. I am not arguing that they should be preserved for the few at the expense of the discomfort of the many, only cautioning that for societies which are already well fed, well clad and well amused, the quest for general higher standards is in certain important respects inevitably self-defeating, and that recognition of this fact should presumably colour their attempts to weigh up present

sacrifices against attainable future benefit. In this respect their problem is a subtler one than that of Viner's countries, where some of the simplest and most straightforward improvements in well-being have yet to be achieved.

(3) Even, however, in most richer countries there is clearly room for improvements of standard in more concrete and humdrum ways; and the next factor which should presumably affect our judgment of what is reasonable in the way of provision for the future is the available evidence on the relation under modern conditions between net capital formation and growth of output. Looking at the course of human history as a whole, and especially of the last two centuries taken as a whole, there seems no reason to doubt the old view that an increase in the ratio of capital stock to output – in Hawtrey's phrase a deepening of capital – has been not merely a symptom but a prime instrument of the enlargement of man's enjoyments and the lightening of his labours. But of recent years in the more advanced countries, we are now told, there has been a change. Invention and research are directed more and more towards the achievement of given results with an economy of material apparatus; devices for the simultaneous transmission of half a dozen messages along a single wire may stand as typical of a great many of the triumphs of modern technology. Viner's countries may still be in the stage where they require the embottlement of large streams of thrift in the bulky basic instruments of power, transport and communication in order to launch themselves on an industrial career or even to rationalise their agriculture. But *my* countries, so it is said, provided they keep their wits about them, ought to be able to provide handsomely for their own futures with the aid of comparatively modest drafts on the net abstinence, voluntary or conscribed, of their citizens. For to the alleged change in technology to which I have just alluded we must add certain facts of a more book-keeping charac-

ter. Not only, in a rapidly advancing economy, are the depreciation quotas being set aside at any moment always in excess of the sums being currently expended for replacement[1] but further, when these sums do come to be spent, they will certainly in most cases be spent in ways which improve as well as merely replacing. During the inflation of recent years, it is agreed, there may have been forces acting in the opposite direction; but taking a long look over the future we can be confident that industry will contrive to make a great deal of material provision for growth which the statistician will not succeed in identifying as 'net investment' requiring to be balanced by 'net saving'.

I hope to hear much discussion of these topics by those in closer touch with the processes of industry in many lands than I am myself. Such discussion will no doubt attach due weight to those rather surprising calculations of Professor Kuznets[2] indicating that in the United States the ratio of reproducible capital to national output, after rising in the forty years following 1879 from the neighbourhood of 3 to the neighbourhood of 4, thereafter ceased to rise, and indeed by 1939 had lost half of the previous advance. It will no doubt endorse Kuznets's strongly emphasised view that in its expenditures on health, education and research, which are not ordinarily classified as 'saving', a modern country is making contributions towards its own future growth which are at least as important as the accumulation of physical instruments. But I hope, too – if I may disclose my own bias – that the disputants will take heed of the possibility that inventions which at their first impact may seem to be 'capital-saving' may prove to be great eaters of capital in the end, just as those which seem to be 'labour-saving' may prove to be

[1] E. D. Domar, 'The Inter-Relation between Capital and Output in the American Economy', *Economic Progress* (Papers and Proceedings of a Round Table, held by the International Economic Association, Louvain 1955), pp. 258–261.

[2] 'Population, Income and Capital', ibid., pp. 36–9 and 46.

great employers of labour. Anyway, so far as the quest for higher standards can be satisfied at all by ampler flows of material goods, it would seem to me that in at any rate the poorer of my richer countries pretty massive embottlements of thrift in such things as strip mills, oil refineries, rejuvenated railway systems, are still likely to be required.

II

Well, having arrived somehow at our hunch – I will not go so far as to call it a judgment – about what we should like to see happening, I suppose the next thing is to set out in order the obstacles which may thwart the fulfilment of our wishes.

(1) First among these I place the danger that the citizens of our richer country will not spontaneously provide enough saving to supplement adequately that which is being done for them, for respectable motives and by respectable means, behind their backs. You will not fail to notice that I have phrased this proposition in somewhat provocative terms; and it does of course cover up a whole string of controversial matters, some of them of so rabbinical a nature as to be unsuitable for exploration in a brief general address of this kind. But I must not run away from making some mention of the major issues involved.

First, what is to be the part played by Government savings, that is, by budget surpluses? I throw out, in order that they may be shot at in debate, some *ballons d'essai* – please remember carefully at this point that we are spending this morning in *my* orchard, not in Viner's. (i) A government can reasonably tax its citizens in order to repay at a reasonable rate debts incurred on their behalf for exceptional purposes such as war. (ii) It can reasonably tax them to defray expenditures on health, education and research which on a broad view contribute to the formation of capital; but it should not as a normal settled policy aim at defraying out of taxation the cost of additional physical capital works except in very special cases. (iii) If the techniques of monetary control have broken down in an inflationary direction, it should accept the resultant windfall budgetary surplus, not give it away, and should even plan to repeat it until the situation is redressed; but it should recognise the situation as one of disease, to be brought to an end as soon as possible.

Next, what is to be the part played by saving done by company directors on behalf of their shareholders? Clearly in my type of country this kind of saving has come to stay on a large scale, and so long as its dimensions are governed by the true needs and prospects of the enterprises concerned, as honestly judged by their responsible heads, it must, in my highly emotive language, be accounted entirely respectable. I suggest that it becomes unrespectable if its dimensions are unduly expanded by the inertia or the inordinate ambitions of particular persons, by the desire of governments to divert the savings to finance their own programmes, by popular pressures to constrict on distributional grounds the flow of money paid out in dividends. For the result of such policies is a distortion of the *character* of the country's capital equipment which may, to say the least of it, go a long way towards cancelling any merits which they may possess in facilitating the desired rate of global growth.

Next, what is to happen if, given 'respectable' savings policies on the part of governments and boards of directors, the spontaneous saving of individuals proves inadequate to implement the desired rate of growth? The first thing to be said in reply is that governments should not suppose that either they, or the company directors under their pressure, can, by making their tax or dividend policies *un*respectable, count on closing the gap. For a point may easily be reached when each extra £1 of thrift so extorted means precious nearly £1 less of thrift spontaneously forthcoming. But it does not follow straight-away that the desired rate of growth need be abandoned. There remains a subtler way of extorting thrift so that it does not appear to be being extorted but to be coming forward spontaneously – a delusion which the magnificent labours of our national income statisticians in recent years have, I believe, done much to fortify in the public mind. The name of this device is inflation, and in case you have not heard of it, I must not filch from Professor Haberler the joy of telling you all about it. Many of us in the past, myself included, have had some words to say in its defence. But it is not such fun as it used to be, for too many people have learnt to dodge its consequences. I am not sure that in Britain the day when the Church of England climbed on to the band-wagon by entering the market for ordinary shares will not be seen in retrospect to have signalised the end of 'a little inflation' as a respectable policy. All I can say is that I should now have to desire a given rate of capital growth very strongly – more strongly than in my 'richer countries' I can see any reason for doing – to be willing to see it consummated with the aid of inflation.

In Britain a few years ago there was a good deal of pessimism about the future of spontaneous individual saving, which appeared to have sunk virtually to zero. Since then there has undoubtedly been a change for the better. But there is now perhaps a tendency for the recorded figures to generate excessive optimism; for so large and varied is the company now assembled on the band-wagon of inflation that it is by no means safe to assume, as is sometimes done, that all the froth savings churned up by the wagon in its career are concentrated in the accounts of the joint stock companies and the Government and that the category labelled 'personal savings' can be regarded as virtually clean thereof. In most of my 'richer countries' the forces making for greater equality in the distribution of net income are extremely strong, and the provision made by the State in aid of personal misfortune (children being counted as misfortunes) very considerable. It seems likely therefore that, if we are resolved to reject the assistance of inflation, there will be need for a good deal of sustained and conscious effort – including the offer of appropriate interest rates – to break down schizophrenia, and ensure harmony between the rate at which the community thinks it would like to grow and the scale on which the individuals composing it are prepared to stoke the fires of growth.

Whether the United States constitutes an exception, of dominating and menacing importance, to this generalisation I must leave to the Conference to discuss. But I should like in this connection to revert for a moment to those Kuznets figures which I mentioned a short time ago. They can be cited as evidence of a decreasing need for thrift in consequence of the change in the character of technical innovation; but they can also be cited as evidence of a constraint placed upon the rate of growth by the limitation of the human propensity to abstinence. For the pendant to that stagnant or declining figure of the ratio of capital stock to output in the United States in recent decades is the figure of a stagnant or declining proportion of annual net income effectively saved. It is interesting that Kuznets's own thoughts seem to veer towards this ultimate explanation of his results: 'On a country-wide scale capital formation is identical *ex post facto* with savings; and limitation of the former proportion (that is, the proportion of capital to output) may in the final analysis be reducible to limitation on the savings proportion, in other words to the spending habits of individuals.'[1]

(2) I pass to another matter which has occasioned anxiety, the character (as distinct from the amount) of

[1] Proceedings of Columbia University Conference on 'National Policy for Economic Welfare at Home and Abroad, p. 41 (Doubleday & Co., New York, 1955).

so much of the thrift nowadays forthcoming in a richer country – safety-seeking, risk-avoiding, and difficult therefore to transmute into industrial capital. This is, I confess, a senior bee in my own bonnet; it is many years since I began to harp on the risk lest in the Anglo-Saxon countries the attractions of the bank deposit, coupled with the strong preference of the banks in favour of lending for short-term working capital purposes, should exercise a chronically depressive influence on the course of fixed capital formation. In the United States in recent years the rise of the so-called term loan seems to signalise something like a revolution in this respect; in Britain it is perhaps regrettable, though inevitable, that the desire of the banks to raise the proportion borne by their riskier assets to the whole back to something like its pre-war level, and the consequent disposition which some of them showed on the morrow of the war to take a more adventurous view of their responsibilities, should have had to be damped down in the overriding interest of curbing inflation. Continental, especially German, banking has suffered from no such inhibitions about the character of its assets, and the lack of them has in the past plunged it into disaster; there the problem takes rather the form of how to create effective capital markets outside the banks, so as to relieve the latter of some of their traditional but perilous tasks.

For of course this is not simply a banking problem; its other facets include the investment policies of the great insurance companies and pension funds, and the excogitation of devices to interest the better-to-do worker in industrial investment without turning him into a reckless addict of the tape-ticker. I have neither the time nor the knowledge to plunge into a sea of institutional detail, and I am conscious of a tendency to split-mind in this matter. But I think what I am trying to suggest is that good may come out of evil; provided the dozen-year-old world-wide inflation itself is terminated and not resumed, the recent scramble for inflation-hedges may turn out to have led to a useful crumbling of certain institutional obstacles to the smooth progress of capital growth.

(3) 'The smooth progress of capital growth!' I have said more so far about the obstacles to growth than about the obstacles to smoothness. Perhaps I have been subconsciously funking to take the plunge, on an occasion of this kind, into the maelstrom of modern trade cycle theory. And even now you will hear from me no stop-press news as to whether the matrix-multiplier does or does not oscillate; no confident judgment as to whether, when we rise from the floor, it is chiefly thanks to the heartbeats of Autonomous Investment, pulsing away in the outhouse in happy oblivion of the world around him, or to Duesenberry Effects governing the consumption of the unemployed, or simply, as I am sometimes tempted to think, to the fortunate fact that with us, as with Dr Johnson's friend who tried to become a philosopher, cheerfulness will keep breaking in. All I can do is to remind you briefly of some of the old snags and the new hopes – just three of each. Among the snags, I still put first, as I did forty years ago, the inevitable lumpiness of the process of investment, so that we cannot make provision for a manifest excess of Tuesday's over Monday's needs without making provision for a presumed excess of Wednesday's needs over Monday's, and in many cases also for a conjectured excess of Wednesday's needs over Tuesday's. Next, the obvious dangers of loss of balance – vertical balance between the several stages of the productive process of a given type of final output; horizontal balance between the different types of final output. Next, and not to be neglected just because in the past some enquirers have failed to dig beneath them for *real* sources of trouble, the contagious forces of over-confidence and gloom.

What about the hopes? In mentioning them I feel obliged to mention also the doubts which make certain things seem to me to *be* causes for hope rather than for confidence or complacency. Avalanches of statistical information, including increasing quantities of that dis-aggregated type of information which is so relevant to the problems of inter-stage and inter-industrial balance, and used to be so difficult to come by. (But is there not, however cunning the devices of pre-digestion employed, some danger of the flair and judgment of executive persons being stunned and paralysed by this very abundance of riches?) Next, as we are told, the increased willingness of great industrial concerns to lay long-ranging plans of growth and stick to them without being dismayed by the threats of transitory recession of demand. (But may not long-run plans which go agley spread more havoc than short-run ones?) Next, the certainty that governments and Central Banks will be ready to take heroic action to prevent recession turning into slump. (But does anybody know for certain how much recession to accept before bringing up the big guns? In America, might not a little more tolerance of recession in 1927 have averted 1929 and therefore 1931–3? Did not Britain perhaps show a little too much alacrity in 1952, Canada in early 1955, to pump up the sagging tyres?)

One need not be a full-blown stagnationist to think it likely that the path of growth is likely to continue to lead through patches of soggy ground – of temporary satura-tion and set-back. One may even perhaps feel that such periods of pause and readjustment are our best protection – and in a humanely organised society a protection not too expensive in terms of individual welfare – against the strong social and political forces making for a continual eating away of the standard of value.

(4) Finally for such small incursion as I propose to make into Professor Lundberg's domain. How far is each of my richer countries, in its efforts to achieve stable progress, likely to be affected, for good or evil, by the

similar efforts of its neighbours? Some, as I started by pointing out, more than others – Britain, for instance, more than the United States. This greater sensitivity of ours to external influences is by no means, as in our more querulous moments we are apt to plead, an unmixed evil. It means that we are apt to be pulled up short in evil courses by balance of payments difficulties, immunity from which might tempt a more self-contained country to press on to the very brink of inflationary disaster. Further, if the penalties of neglecting the warnings of the foreign exchanges are in our case more severe, the rewards of paying them due heed may also be richer. In a self-contained country the risk that measures to check inflation may generate an uncontrollable spiral of deflation may well be greater than in a country whose level of activity depends largely on her foreign connections, and to whom therefore, provided she looks carefully to her costs, the buoyancy of world demand may render powerful assistance in setting a floor to any malign deflationary process. Exposure to all the winds that blow means exposure to fair winds as well as foul.

Nevertheless, the fact that, for whatever underlying reasons, the different richer countries are capable of different rates of growth is bound, in my view, to be a source of certain embarrassments. To dismiss these embarrassments as 'purely monetary' is not, I think, helpful: for, even if it were always true, the monetary measures needed to avert them may themselves be of such a kind as to contribute to instability. If productivity is increasing faster in A than in B, that may involve a choice between A taking her reward more largely in the form of rising money incomes and less largely in the form of falling prices than is healthy from the point of view of her own stability: or alternatively, imposing on B a flexibility of exchange rates which, whatever the academic arguments in favour of such a régime, works out badly in its effects on the stability of B.

Moreover, it has been shown that these difficulties are *not* always 'purely monetary'. If the difference between national rates of productivity growth is itself differential between different branches of productive activity, strains may be imposed on the adaptive capacities of the weaker countries which impair their stability and inhibit their growth. I do not think there is any way to avoid these troubles except by a retreat into isolationism which would be worse than the disease. But they seem to make it all the more desirable that the richer richer countries should refrain from adding to the difficulties of the poorer richer countries by adhering tenaciously to lines of production in which the verdict of Lord Justice Comparative Cost has been decisively given against them. I have no doubt that Viner will wish to extend this reflection to cover *his* countries as well. When he has done so, we academic persons can have a pleasant time during the intervals of our debates inveighing against the misdeeds in this field of each others' Ministries of Agriculture and Commerce. We can but trust that their activities will not be so misguided as to hamper us too severely in our difficult task of growing at the right pace to the right size, and so, like Alice, finding ourselves 'at last in the beautiful garden, among the bright flower-beds and the cool fountains'.[1]

[1] Op. cit., p. 100.

II

THOUGHTS ON INFLATION[1]

It is for me a great and unexpected honour to be invited to attend this birthday party, and in such very distinguished company. My thoughts inevitably go back to a sultry evening in Chicago fourteen years ago, when it fell to my lot, as a very minor cog in the British Treasury machine, to join with an American colleague in explaining to a polite, but I think rather puzzled, gathering of Federal Reserve Bank directors how desirable it was that some kind of international monetary institution should be brought to birth before the end of the war. Our task was rendered somewhat delicate by the fact that our respective superiors were by no means yet in agreement as to what the shape and function of this unborn child should be. But in spite of that, and in spite of the heat, it was a very pleasant evening; and in due course the child was born, and turned out to be twins. One of them has always been a sturdy, steady-going fellow; the other at times perhaps has looked a bit pale and ill at ease. But today, at any rate, both are in bouncing health, and it is a pleasure and honour to be their guest, not now in any official or semi-official capacity whatever, but as an ordinary citizen representing nobody but himself.

It is, however, as I understand it, not the functions and problems of the international twins themselves which form the theme of this afternoon's discussion, but rather those of the Monetary Authorities of the several nations whom they exist to comfort and to serve; for the twins are

[1] An address delivered at the open session of the joint annual meeting of the International Monetary Fund and the International Bank for Reconstruction and Development, in Washington, September 25, 1957.

*inter*national not *super*national organs, and the primary responsibility for creating an environment in which they can function usefully lies not with them but with the authorities of the member nations. And what a mixed bag of nations we are! Rich nations a bit worried about the implications of their recent spectacular rates of growth, and poor nations wondering how they are ever to grow at all, except in respect of the number of mouths to be fed. Nations in which the odd habit of paying direct taxes is well established, others in which it is perhaps in some danger of erosion; others, again, in which it is still rather an unfamiliar idea. New nations in which monetary management is felt to be difficult because of the absence of an outside capital market, and old nations in which it is arguable that management would now really be easier if certain time-honoured excrescences of the banking system should be found to have withered away. Nations in which the relations between Treasury and Central Bank are conducted beneath a blaze of arc lights, and nations in which they belong to the class of ineffable mysteries into which it is impious to pry.

Inevitably, while I represent nobody but myself, such thoughts as I have to utter will betray what I will call my upper-middle-class national origin. I belong to a country where the standard of life is high, but not so high that there is any difficulty in seeing how it could be improved; and where, whatever the remote future may hold, the problem for a good while to come seems likely to be to find in the breasts of its individual citizens enough energy and thrift to bring to birth anything like all the projects on which collectively they think they have set their hearts. A country rich enough to abjure the extremes of economic nationalism and to play a reasonable part in the development of the world outside, but cursed or blessed, unlike some others, with a healthy balance of payments problem calculated to pull it up sharply – if not always quite sharply enough – when it indulges in fits of unwarranted extravagance at home or over-ambitious expansion or largesse overseas.

No doubt, I say, my slant on all these monetary problems is affected by my country of origin as well as by my personal make-up. It may be, to be more specific, that I should feel more complacent about the decline in the value of the monetary unit which seems to be everywhere in progress if I could regard it, as some respected authorities in the United States appear to do, as an incidental and relatively innocuous by-product of a perpetual process of boost necessary to prevent a rich country from slipping over the precipice of satiety into the morass of stagnation; or if I could regard it, as I think some of the leaders and advisers of underdeveloped countries do, as a rather regrettable but nevertheless essential ingredient of a policy designed to enable a poor country to achieve the maximum of growth in the minimum of time. But for a West European country in present circumstances I regard the slide of the currency as unequivocally an evil; and it is on the assumption that it *is* an evil – and personally, in spite of what I said just now, I regard that assumption as being valid for North America as well – that I should like to say a little about some of the reasons for which we have all become ensnared so distressingly in its toils.

One reason, I think, is the protean variety of forms which the age-old conflict between the King and the Coiner can take under modern conditions. Assuming for the moment the King to be a good King, and to desire to provide his loving subjects with a sufficiency, and no more, of sound money for their use, there are several ways, less crude than the crucible and the graving-tool, in which his loving subjects can thwart his good intentions. The history of banking legislation is largely the history of the King's struggle to recapture the prerogative of money-creation which the London goldsmiths in the seventeenth century discovered how to steal – a struggle in which the balance of social advantage has by no means always been on one side, and which has eventuated in the bankers' money being as indubitably money as the King's money is. But even when the King has got the bankers under his thumb, what exactly is a bank and what is only just not a bank? What is money, and what is only just not money but only a claim to money? No wonder if the conscientious central banker sometimes feels like an earlier Per, Peer Gynt, contending with his mysterious enemy, the Boyg:

'He is there! And there! And he's round the corner!
Name who you are! . . . all slimy, misty,
Not so much as a shape! It's as bad as a battle
In a cluster of snarling half-wakened bears'

– only perhaps, in times of booming trade and high employment, all the bears are bulls – except indeed so far as government securities are concerned.

Add to this the age-old power of the public – and a public which in 1945 in many lands found itself wallowing in pools of King's money, bankers' money, near-money – to vary the speed at which the precious stuff passes from hand to hand, and we can all agree that even if the game had been a straight battle of wits between what I have called the Virtuous King and the Coiner, the task of Authority these last twelve years would not have been an easy one. And thereby hang, of course, all sorts of detailed issues of policy which I can do no more than notice. For instance, ought Authority to be content with general powers of quantitative control, or ought it to exercise if it possesses, and to acquire if it does not possess, the right to exert more refined and particular pressures? On these matters my own inexpert opinion lies somewhere in the middle of the road, all ready to be kicked about accordingly. I have read with high respect, but I think with regret, the careful statement in which a very important central banking authority indeed has recently disclaimed

the desire to be re-entrusted with those special powers for
the regulation of consumer instalment credit which have
undoubtedly been found useful elsewhere. On the other
hand, on reflection I share with a reviewer in the *Economist*
newspaper some malaise at the gusto with which a much
respected British authority on 'Do's and Don't's for
Central Banks', my old pupil Professor Sayers, has been
recommending those organs in the newer countries to be
fertile in seeking out particular sectors where the shoe can
be made to pinch especially hard.

Rather than get entangled in such important but
specialist issues I will ask leave to use my time in sticking
out my neck on one or two broader problems. When all is
said that can be said about near-money and speeded-up
money, it is no use pretending that all the trouble about
inflation has been due to the struggle between King and
Coiner. More often than not it has also been a matter of
the King stabbing himself in the back, or at all events
setting snares for his own feet. In the last few years some
of our member governments have been running current
deficits. Others have been skirmishing nearer the edge
in this respect that one might have hoped would seem
good to them in such piping times. Others again have
collected current surpluses from their citizens on a scale
which would have seemed incredible only twenty years
ago, but have used these surpluses not for the repayment
of debt but towards the financing of large and often
inherently admirable projects of capital development; and
frequently the money collected in taxes has had to send
out an SOS for some created money to help it in its task.
Nearly everywhere, whether or not themselves deeply
implicated in the actual process of what the blue books
call fixed capital formation, governments – at all events
till quite recently – have felt impelled, in the sacred names
of development, growth and full employment, to afford it
the utmost encouragement within their power.

As a result the world is much more richly supplied with the instruments of well-being than it was twelve years ago, even if, in spite of the efforts of our host the I.B.R.D., the geographical spread of this great accession of wealth has been uneven. But there has been a price to be paid. For a sustained whirlwind of enterprise, activity and optimism of this kind necessarily generates an upward pressure on what economists call the equilibrium prices of the several hired factors of production. And the thesis which I want to put before you is this: that the sociological climate of the times has been such that in the case of one of these factors – capital – the pressure of effective demand has been unduly resisted, while in the case of the other – labour – it has found a kindred pressure rising up to meet and coalesce with it, and that the result in both cases has been to intensify the inflationary fever which in some measure every period of rapid expansion has always brought in its train.

To make my point, *j'accuse*, generally and, if you like, wildly, without attempting to make any of the qualifications which a scholarly inquiry into the history of the last duodeni – no, duodecennium, a period as you see whose very name carries a flavour of morbid inflammation·– might show to be required. I suggest that almost always and everywhere the powers that be have been too slow to recognise the complete transformation which has been wrought in the world's capital markets by what I will call the Growth Spirit, and have moved to meet it by steps too little and too late. There are always many reasons impelling governments to sit on the head of the rate of interest – reasons of prestige, of budgetary equilibrium, in some cases of balance of payments equilibrium. These reasons are naturally at their maximum strength with governments to whom war has brought monstrous accretions of debt, while victory precludes the simple solution of repudiation. And these common-sense forces of resistance to higher interest rates have derived sustenance and support not only from the sociological climate to which I have just alluded but from subtleties of economic theory which, while illuminating up to a point, have spread darkness as well as light. For they have worked to create excessive scepticism about the broad lines of causation which my great predecessor, Alfred Marshall, seventy years ago summarised for the benefit of a Royal Commission puzzled, like so many of its successors in various lands, by the complexities of the relations between causes and effects, between interest and prices, between long rates and short. 'My position' – so runs the passage to which I refer – 'is that the mean rate of discount is governed by the mean rate of interest for long loans; and that again is determined by the extent and richness of the field for the investment of capital on the one hand, and on the other by the amount of capital seeking investment.'

Surely that is still the basic truth; and surely, without being impossibly purist or hypercritical, we can and must give heed to the danger that if governments do not see fit to pay rather higher rates of interest because capital is scarce they may have to pay much higher rates of interest in a desperate attempt to keep pace with the foreseen depreciation of money. There have been some disquieting portents in my country in the last few months, including a strange vision, sponsored by a great political party, of the whole army of present and prospective old-age pensioners scrambling, under the guidance of a government-appointed trustee, on to that band-wagon of the equity market, whither so many colleges, churches and the like have already found their way. How right and desirable that some of those who save should, to the extent that their circumstances permit, face the uncertainties, and therefore on balance enjoy the profits, of industrial enterprise! But what a perversion of true principle, what a 'worst corruption of the best', when gilt-edged and

equities change hats, and what should be a considered taking of chances in the hopes of additional reward becomes a disorderly scramble for cover from foreseen and tolerated spoliation!

So let us hope to see soaring markets for public and private debt again some day, but when, and not until, we can be sure that they signify not only an abundance of private saving but a restored and a justified confidence on the part of humble and cautious people that those who have promised to keep their savings safe will really do so. It is early to judge, but I do believe that in my own country, as a result of the resolute action recently taken, the prospects of that day's dawning are much brighter than they were only a week ago.

So much for the price of capital. Now what about the price of labour? Here the economic stalactite of inflated demand has met a sociological stalagmite of upthrusting claims; and when stalactite and stalagmite meet and fuse in an icy kiss – I hope there is no geologist present to tell me I am talking through my hat – nobody on earth can be quite sure just where the one ends and the other begins. My own disposition has been quite definitely to emphasise the superior role of inflated demand, and to believe therefore that a sustained pressure of monetary and budgetary restraint *can* work its way through on to the labour markets and effectively promote the making of bargains which do not outrage the community's fundamental interest in safeguarding the value of its money. I think that in some countries this process *has* now been set to work and that in spite of some initial disappointments it is far too early to write it off as a forlorn hope.

Some of us have felt bound to point out that if such pressures are inadequately applied or prematurely relaxed, the most eloquent adjurations of governments to their citizens to behave themselves are bound to fall on deaf ears. 'Better,' as a Very High Authority once remarked to a certain Eastern king, 'to die in the discharge of one's own duty; the duty of another is full of peril.'[1] But I would not wish to deny that in this matter as in others truth has two sides, or at any rate one side and a half. The habit of demanding large and frequent increases in monetary rewards grows by what it feeds on, and may be found to linger on after, as a result of the successful application of monetary and fiscal pressures, justification for it in the technical state of the labour market has passed away. Economic forces, as my teacher Pigou has reminded us, 'operate upon human beings, not upon electrical machines of perfect sensibility'. Nobody, therefore, can guarantee that an ebbing of the high tide of inflated demand will not, unless wise counsels prevail, lay bare rocks of inflated wage claims, which will lead to industrial strife if denied and to loss of trade and consequent unemployment if conceded, unemployment for which the prime responsibility would then lie not upon those who have done their duty in safeguarding the standard of value but upon those who have got into the habit of opening their mouths unreasonably wide.

In the past the termination of periods of acute inflation has often involved a 'stabilisation crisis' of greater or less intensity. In seeking to implement as smooth a transition as possible from the much milder, yet potentially lethal, epidemic of inflation which has struck the western world, no fiscal or monetary authority which is faithfully doing its own job need, I think, be ashamed to ask and to accept the support of those who think and speak more naturally in moral than in economic terms, and who feel it in their bones that, while the seats of economic power may change from age to age, what does not change is that

> 'O, it is excellent
> To have a giant's strength; but it is tyrannous
> To use it like a giant.'

---

[1] *Bhagavad-Gîtâ*, III, 35.